Homes and Gardens

INTRODUCTION TO ANTIQUES

by Therle Hughes

illustrations by Hussein Abbo

Printed in Great Britain by C. Nicholls & Company Ltd.

Contents

FOREWORD

Therle Hughes, the author of this book, needs no introduction to the readers of *Homes and Gardens*, to which magazine she has been contributing regularly for many years. She has always been a writer and is a recognised authority on English antiques with ten books to her credit on a wide variety of subjects ranging from *Prints for the Collector* and *English Needlework* to a number on various aspects of antique furniture. She has also collaborated with her husband, G. Bernard Hughes, and together they have produced other books on our rich heritage of fine craftsmanship in many different mediums. The son of a Berlin sculptor, Hussein Abbo, who illustrates her text, has had a varied career. Having studied art in this country, Greece and Rome, his experience includes being an architectural assistant, restoring ceramics at the Victoria and Albert Museum and welding heavy metal for pre-fabricated buildings. He was working for a manufacturing silversmith when he won an award for his Topham Trophy design. *Homes and Gardens* recently brought these two talents together and the successful combination of informative text and meticulously researched and finely executed drawings aroused so much interest both at home and abroad, that we decided to bring this partnership to an even wider public by producing this our first book. We are confident that it will add to the knowledge and pleasure of the rapidly growing numbers of people who delight in the whole world of antiques.

THE EDITOR

1. *FURNITURE*

Seldom can anyone put an exact date upon an antique furnishing. Indeed, a date on it would immediately be suspect! Yet even beginners find, surprisingly enough, that innumerable details of design, materials, ornament and manufacturing techniques are deciding for them almost subconsciously whether a period piece is "right".

This chapter outlines a few of the more important details to help in understanding and dating antique English furniture. Fashions changed slowly, of course, and overlapped. Lavish notions were drastically modified to meet yeoman home-making. But, throughout, all the traditions of fine furniture craftsmanship lasted far into the days of Victorian mass-production.

Mid 16th to mid 17th century: how it all began. Some grand furniture remains from Tudor days – straight-backed, panelled armchairs, extending "draw" tables, carved and panelled bedsteads. Medieval carpenters had knocked up chests and benches of hammered planks but Tudor joiners perfected the all-important mortise and tenon joint characteristic of this period's "joined" and panelled furniture and

---

Below: walnut desk, c. 1725. Right: mid 17th c. gate table with bobbin turning and late 16th c. mortised drawtop table.

witnessed by the now slightly projecting heads of their wooden dowel pins.

At this time, too, the turner added massive swelling ornament to his lathe-shaped bedposts, table legs and the like; these were often carved in cup-and-cover designs. Many of these early examples of furniture were painted, some decorated with simple inlays and great use was made of elegant iron handles and hinges.

This was followed by the extraordinary contrasts of the 17th century. Folding gateleg tables for parlour dining had smaller, single (armless) chairs. Even hugger-mugger storage in deep chests was improved by including drawers in the so-called mule chest.

Carved ornament might be reduced to shallow repetition of lunette or guilloche pattern, but pride in good workmanship was expressed in carefully mitred, deeply moulded panels and orderly turned ornament such as ball-and-reel outlines to chair and table legs, left square, of course, for all joints. Seats might be covered in leather or the woollen pile known as turkey work.

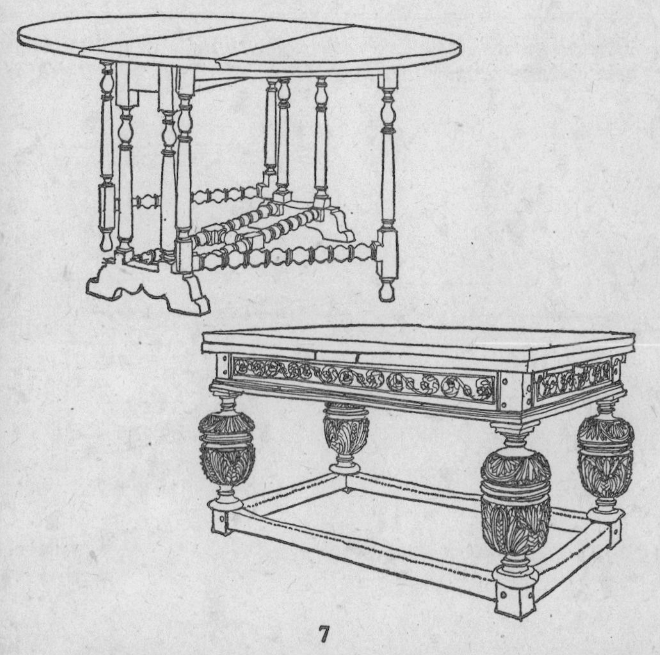

1660s to 1700s: the rise of the cabinet maker. When Charles II and his court returned from their exile on the Continent in 1660, they naturally required the ornate furniture of the cabinet-maker. This was a turning point. For the first time construction was marked by a smooth, glued-on surface or veneer. This thin wood could be chosen for beauty regardless of strength, walnut being most popular including knotty burr-wood.

Sometimes the wooden veneer was applied to the furniture in symmetrical patterns of contrasting grains (which was known as parquetry). More elaborately, fragments of veneer in contrasting colours were fitted together so that they made attractive patterns (known as marquetry) of

---

Chest of drawers, c. 1685, top and drawer fronts decorated with marquetry patterned veneers, simple brass drop handles.

flowers and birds or, at a later date, intricate scrolling.

Chests of drawers and bureaux showed a new delicacy in such details as drawer dovetails and the earliest brass drop handles. The early tall cabinet-on-stand was rectangular with straight cornice and swelling frieze above cabinet doors or a fall front and a dozen small drawers, perhaps, around the central cupboard.

Other specialist craftsmen set up as carvers and gilders making ornate furniture such as stands for luxury cabinets of oriental lacquer. Some gilded and silvered furniture was patterned in low relief with gesso composition for wall mirrors and delicate-legged side tables.

Even the humble turner had to learn to extend his skill,

Below: Stuart cabinet-on-stand with swelling frieze above. Right: tall chair with barley sugar twist and caned panels.

and a conspicuous detail characteristic of late Stuart chairs – especially armchairs – and small tables is the swash-turned or barley sugar twist.

New features in late Stuart times include comfortable panels of caning in the seat and in the framework of the backward sloping back.

Carving on the broad back is often a pattern of leafy scrolls, perhaps with "boys" supporting a crown. This is repeated in another new feature, a broad ornamental stretcher high-set between the front legs. In the last decade of the century, "William and Mary" chairs tended to have S scrolls cresting the tall back, supporting the sagging arms and also serving as massive front legs.

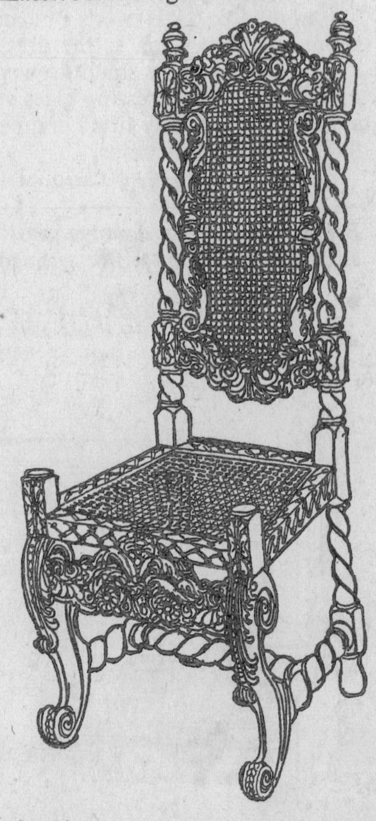

1700s to 1720s: Queen Anne grace. Queen Anne reigned only from 1702 until 1714, but the style associated with her name changed only gradually in George I's reign. There was a new demand for occasional furniture – fashionable walnut still in solid and veneer – and a new care for its convenience and graceful detail.

The period's appealing love of curves runs from the arching tops of mirror and cabinet through the comfortable, shoulder-fitting walnut chair back to the bold, rounded knee and incurving taper of the cabriole leg. This leg design is interesting as it quickly escaped the restrictions of cross stretchers, save in such new upholstered luxuries as winged high-backed armchairs and early sofas.

Fashionable beds were immensely tall but other bedroom furniture, such as the dressing table with an arched kneehole flanked by small drawers, looks delightful in any room today. The dressing glass with supports mounted on a small stand of tiny fitted compartments would have been flanked by candle-stands.

At the same time, occasional tables were usually made

Below: arch-topped dressing glass, c. 1710, occasional table, bended back chair. Right: gate table on cabrioles, c. 1725.

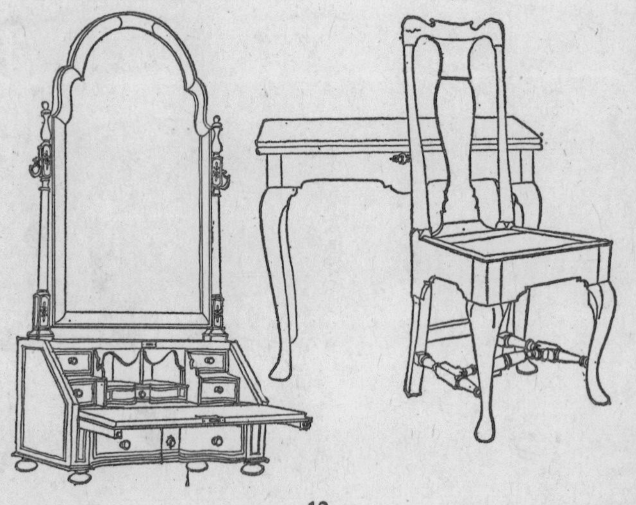

specifically for card playing or writing, losing the elegant curved stretchers of the 17th century's end in favour of free-standing cabrioles. A scroll-footed pole screen would be an obvious accompaniment. Delight in oriental lacquer continued with English imitations known as japanning, including superb long case clocks.

1720s to 1750s: early Georgian vigour. Escallop shell carving on walnut, trade mark as it were of the previous period, continued into early Georgian days (purely for convenience dated 1720 to 1750). But the up and coming wood was mahogany, dark, heavy and so dense that it was both the pride and despair of the woodcarvers.

Details such as ball-and-claw feet and eagle-head chair arm terminals, laboriously carved in the early "Spanish" or "San Domingo" mahogany have retained an almost metallic vigour and crispness.

The huge tree girth meant that a single plank could serve as each flap of a large folding table, supported by a single hinged leg. This gate table was free of the stretchers that cluttered the older gateleg table. At the same time a

new delicacy could be introduced in pierced work. Chairs changed from the rounded, arched back supporting a central splat in simple baluster outline to designs with a cupid's bow cresting rail making a sharp angle with its side supports and enclosing a boldly pierced and carved splat.

William Kent (1686 to 1748) and his followers designed massive furniture in the manner of their classical "Palladian" architecture such as heavy console tables.

But the period is above all remembered for such unpretentious pleasures as the corner chair, conveniently shaped for card players, and the reading chair for a man to straddle and display silk coat tails.

Early Georgian chair: ball-and-claw feet, cupid's bow cresting rail. Beautifully worked long case clock of the 1720s.

1750 to 1760: mid Georgian gaiety. It is still possible to find a mansion with state rooms furnished in the full magnificence of the mid 18th century's wonderful pierced and carved mahogany, ranging from tables and chairs to the elegant little three-legged washbasin stand for the hair-powdering closet, now sometimes misnamed a wig-stand. Adding colour to mahogany in solid and veneer, cabinet-makers might use oriental lacquer and European japanning for such handsome drawing room pieces as the low set of drawers, often enclosed in wide cupboard doors, then known as a commode.

Furniture made at this period is often dubbed Chippendale because Thomas Chippendale brought out the first

---

Below: Chinese Chippendale chair with lattice back, straight-legs. Right: rococo mirror frame in Ince and Mayhew style.

edition of his important *Gentleman and Cabinet Maker's Director* in 1754. This offered the furniture trade a wide range of designs. Reproductions of these may be by contemporaries or later copyists, but known work by the Chippendale firm followed later fashions.

For minor rooms, this period indulged in uninhibited romantic gaiety, its asymmetrical scrolling ornament full of minor incident, from waterfalls and columns to Chinamen and pagodas. "Chinese" and "Gothic" ornament prompted some unusual furniture – "Chinese" chairs with lattice backs and straight, pierced legs and "Gothic" with church window shaping and cluster column legs.

Chippendale's lesser rivals included Ince and Mayhew

who published their *Universal System of Household Furniture*, 1759 to 1762. Use of richly grained Cuban mahogany led to decorative panelling once more, for cabinets that might be partly glazed with the period's improved crown glass and slender mahogany glazing bars.

Pillar-and-claw furniture was never better, with three crisply carved cabriole legs supporting a turned and carved pillar and an adjustable firescreen, perhaps, or a circular table top. The most familiar – and the most reproduced – table has its rim carved in a series of curves and sharp angles known as a piecrust. Brass bail handles for drawers became stronger, with boldly pierced back plates.

1760s to 1780: the mellow mood of neo-classicism. Architect Robert Adam (1728 to 1792) designed many furnishings to suit his mansions and his admiration for the classic world led to the neo-classic vogue. Furniture was designed for contemporary requirements but with deference to classical ideals, in attractively proportioned, geometrical shapes with ornament flat or in low relief. Everything had to be cleanly symmetrical: the favourite

Below: Adam sideboard table flanked by urns on pedestals. Right: mirror with sphinx ornament and folding piecrust table.

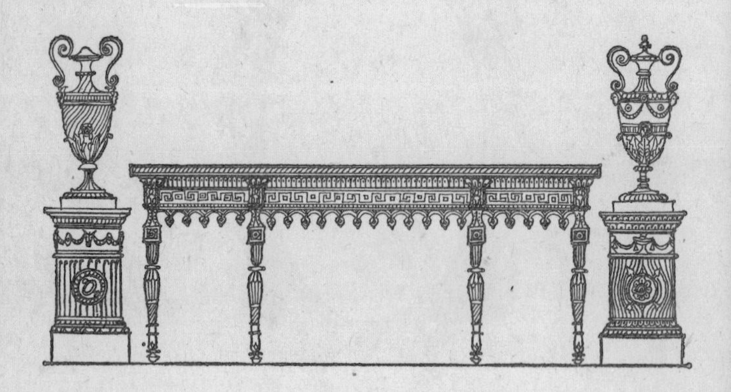

outline was the bland oval medallion or the pointed-end, shuttle shaped ellipse, for panels, mirror frames, chair backs, even the machine-stamped backplates of drawer handles.

Enrichment was detail taken from classic ornament: urns, swags of drapery, pendulous bell flowers and husks, saucer-like circular paterae, the anthemion or stylised honeysuckle flower, and much vertical fluting known as reeding, which suited the period's tapering straight legs.

All this is found in mahogany, ranging from the magnificent flame-grained Cuban variety to the cheaper Honduras (baywood) in solid and veneer. Even country work in oak and native fruit woods might be banded with mahogany to add an uneasy touch of fashion.

Mahogany contrasted splendidly with gilded furnishings such as hanging mirror frames of wood and composition and the familiar lyre-back chair, but Adam's somewhat effeminate designs especially suited the pale golden colour and marvellous silky grain of satinwood.

This in its turn might be banded with exotic kingwood

or tulip wood, but in the 1770s such extravagance – on a drawing room commode, perhaps – called for neo-classical figures painted in the style of Angelica Kauffmann or medallions in delicate coloured marquetry. Cheaper substitutes included wood painted all over in a pale shade. Wedgwood's figure plaques in matt-surfaced jasper ware were mounted on cabinet furniture of the 1780s.

Another important "name" is George Hepplewhite. Nothing is known of his own work but his *Cabinet Maker and Upholsterer's Guide* was first published in 1788, two years after his death. This shows a charmingly homely interpretation of neo-classicism with a simple flowing serpentine grace, from the gently undulating pediment to

Tall cabinet in Hepplewhite-style neo-classicism with simple swags on glass doors and smoothly out-curving "French" feet.

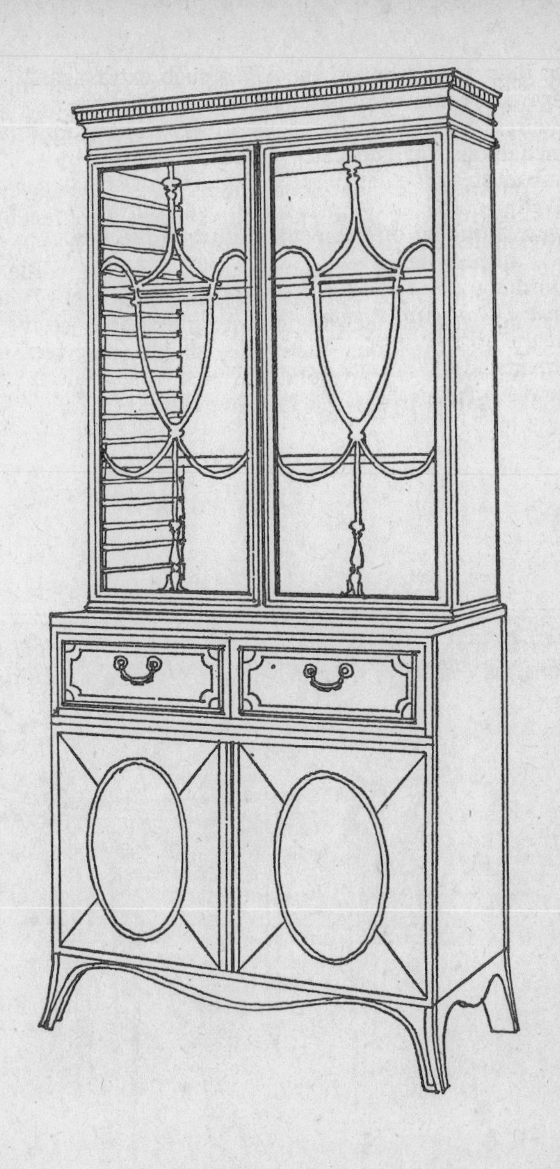

the smoothly out-curving "French" feet. A contemporary, Thomas Shearer, is associated with designs in the anonymous and often reissued *Cabinet Maker's London Book of Prices*, another influential trade manual.

Collectable dining room items include brass-banded mahogany plate pails and wine cisterns and the butler's tray on its folding stand. But the choice is endless, including the pleasant little Pembroke table, hanging corner cupboards and cabinets with elegant patterns of slender glazing bars, by such important large scale manufacturers as George Seddon. Victorians shared our pleasure in "Hepplewhite" chairs but distorted the proportions of those shield shaped backs and tapering legs.

Below: neo-classic Pembroke table. Right: Sheraton chairs show the transition from neo-classic grace to solid Regency.

1790s to 1800s: the Sheraton view of furnishing. Poor Thomas Sheraton (1751 to 1806) died in poverty but now is renowned for the style of furniture recorded in his pattern books, especially in his *Cabinet Maker and Upholsterer's Drawing Book*, published 1791 to 1794. In many ways, his designs for light cabinet work and squarer chairs show a transition between the sweeping curves and serpentine shaping of waning neo-classic grace and the heavy square solidity of the Regency's typical Greco-Roman-Etruscan styles.

No work by him is known but his designs often have a personal, womanly charm. He accepted the period's drastic economies, with recourse to poorer wood and cheaply

painted ornament, but his designs are often full of ingenuity at a time when men and women had a liking for contrivances like movable desk fitments, elaborate, pouched work tables, adjustable mirrors and firescreens. His Carlton House table desk has never gone out of production.

Another late 18th century desk, the tambour or reed top, had a flexible, rounded lid composed of narrow laths glued horizontally on to stiff fabric, its ends controlled in grooved runners. A sideboard might have a central tambour cupboard. Sheraton shared his period's pleasure in neat little feet to much light, delicate furniture, such as thimble toes on tapering, turned legs and great use of brass castors. On pillar-and-claw furniture like tiered dumb waiters and

Below: the Carlton House table desk has never gone out of production. Right: square-ended, bow-front chest of drawers.

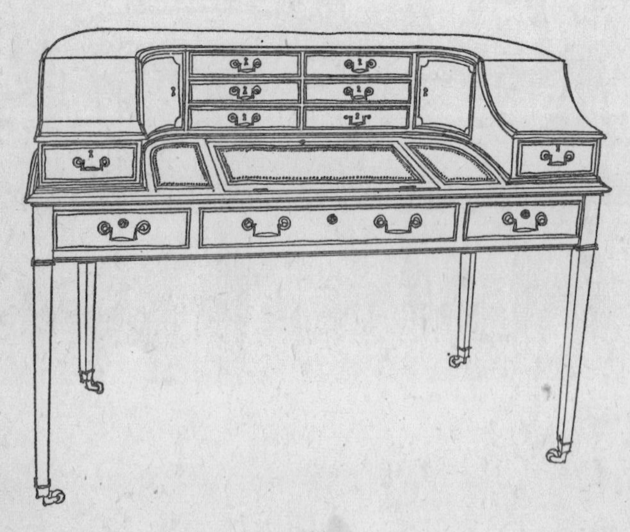

the individual tea tables called teapoys, the claw legs tend to be very slender in a sagging outline.

Plainer, squarer outlines are seen in square-ended, bow-fronted chests of drawers and drawing room commodes. A chair might be cane-seated again, the back supports topped with an ornamental panel above a central pattern of cross-bars, high jutting arms adding to a high-shouldered effect. Many comfortable windsor chairs date to this period, even when their legs retain the old cabriole outline. These splendid country chairs were made to stand endless rough handling on flagstone floors. The saddle seat was thick enough to be drilled with holes to support the hooped back and out-jutting legs.

1800 to 1820s: Regency style. A scroll-ended sofa, a long, narrow sofa-table with folding flaps at the ends instead of the sides, a jaunty little chair with scimitar legs rounding out back and front in simple concave curves from seat to floor – we all know some of the characteristics of down-to-earth Regency furnishings, far too abundant still to have been restricted to the Regency years, which were actually 1811 to 1820.

The style had its beginnings in the 1790s when a deeper archaeological interest in the classical world prompted imitation of couches, chairs and the like rather than the 18th century's invention and superficial ornament. Napoleon's campaigns, and the 1802 peace, started enthusiasm

Below: Regency sofa-table with scroll brackets and inlaid ornament. Right: a cane-seated chair with scimitar legs.

for sheathed caryatid figures, winged lions, lotus buds and other striking Egyptian detail.

There are many collectable pieces in the trestle (horse) style, such as long dressing glasses, games tables with reversible tops and pouch work tables. Other attractive Regency items include canterbury sheet music stands, banner firescreens and the small square desk which was known as a davenport.

Fashionable brass ornament meant increasingly ornate inlays, galleries, grilles, feet (often with castors), including the ubiquitous lion with a ring in its mouth. Glass knob handles were soon followed by attractive flat wooden ones in the 1820s and some of painted china.

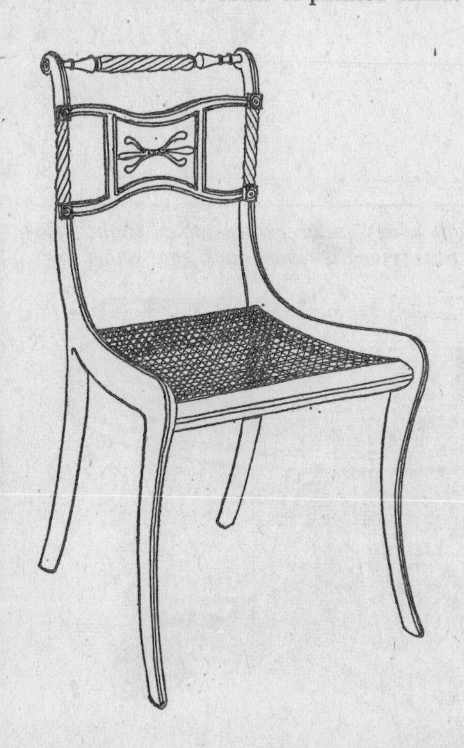

1820s to 1830s: late Georgian contrasts. This period is squeezed in between Regency and Victorian and sometimes known as Biedermeier. Regency fashions now tended to become clumsy and florid while attempting early 18th century French gaiety. Typical is the broad "Greek" front leg spoiling the proportions of a low, swept-back Regency chair. Also unwelcome, perhaps, was the increasing use of french polishing to give a highly vulnerable gloss. But this period saw too the introduction of easy-to-live-with balloon-backed chairs, as well as extremely cheap, hard-wearing, mass-produced kitchen chairs (white Wycombes). Its contrasts include "Gothic" solemnity and the scrolling gaiety of papier mâché furnishings.

Below: late Georgian heavy pillar centre table. Right: neo-Elizabethan chair has typically long back and short legs.

1837 to 1855: early Victoriana. Papier mâché furniture is a particularly endearing detail of the crowded early Victorian scene. Firescreens, small tables, teapoys, workboxes and especially trays are to be found in varying qualities of this ware, its gleaming, varnished ornament fixed by slow stoving and long hand polishing.

Its restless curving shapes were acclaimed as revived rococo or "Louis XV", its gay, all-over patterns including shimmering mother of pearl. But this is only one feminine ghost of a period that took itself very seriously.

Another was romantic Gothic, with beds, chairs, even the popular nesting tables adorned with "church window" architectural features. This escapism is most attractive,

perhaps, as individual touches in arching cabinet doors or galleried writing table.

This clinging to the safety of earlier styles is seen again in somewhat ungainly suites of furniture that Victorians dubbed Elizabethan, although their characteristics such as twist turning had been introduced a century later.

These may still confuse beginner collectors until they recognise the long-back-and-short-leg proportions of much Victorian furniture, taken to extremes in their favourite prie-dieu chair. This chair was popular as a way of showing off the home embroiderer's cross-stitch in Berlin wools, common from the 1830s as a phase of the period's story-telling pictures and naturalistic flower ornament – recorded, too, in many a firescreen and footstool. Crude aniline dyes came only in the 1850s.

In its padded upholstery the chair expressed the very human pleasure in comfort, in the reassurance of plump, fabric-smothered, circular ottoman and two-person sociable sofa. Ever-increasing numbers of middle class homes made huge demands on furniture craftsmen of all grades

Below: comfortable button-back sofa and iron conservatory chair. Right: Eastlake cabinet, and chiffonnier, c. 1870.

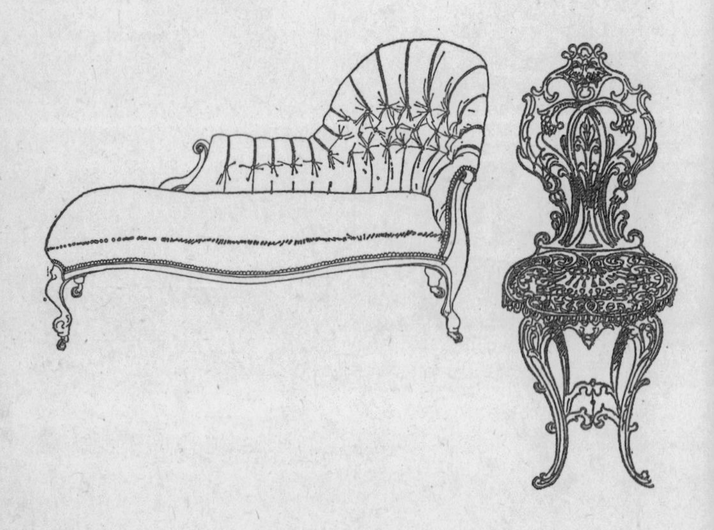

and collectors can only be thankful that much shoddy work has disintegrated and that more remains with beautifully fitting drawers and doors fine dovetailed joints, well, turned wooden knobs from a period that still chose rosewood for the drawing room, mahogany for dining.

1850s to 1870s: the assertive mid Victorians. Walnut, today regarded as most Victorian of woods, was largely a mid-Victorian drawing room taste, with oak then for dining. But this time of assertive, substantial furniture is a confusion of styles, built to last and long treasured for its abundance of surface ornament.

Marquetry patterns are found on wood and in the brass and tortoiseshell ornament imitated in England from an old French process and called boulle or buhl. Tunbridge ware marquetry was popular in mosaic patterns of tiny squares forming picturesque views and other pictorial scenes in the Berlin wool manner.

Mid-Victorian exhibitions showed huge pieces of ostentatious elaboration. Fine craftsmanship defied cheap imitation like the popular painted wood graining and

shallow machine-cut carving. But it fostered reaction towards simplicity expressed by William Morris's associates from the 1860s. Minor pieces most likely to appeal to today's collectors range from spindled corner whatnots to iron conservatory seats and tables and familiar rush-seated "Morris" chairs and settees inspired by Sussex country designs.

Another familiar favourite that became very popular in the 1860s was plain bentwood furniture, such as round-backed chairs with cane seats and slender out-curving legs.

1880s to 1900: late Victorian contradictions. Collectors who dismiss the late Victorian era for much shoddy, ill-designed pieces should realise that several important

Below: Eaton Hall upholstered tub chair. Right: popular from 1860s, bentwood rocker features rounded back and caned seat.

artists and designers, like C. L. Eastlake and B. J. Talbert, were attempting to counteract shabby commercialism, mainly by urging a return to medieval ideas of straightforward hand craftsmanship enriched with imaginative ornament. The phrase arts and crafts covers a wide range of effort towards "making useful things, making them well and making them beautiful," as declared by C. R. Ashbee. Designers like Ernest Gimson relied on balanced design expressed in fine quality woods by expert cabinet-makers and enriched with metal mounts.

For those with no interest in minor handicraft movements, the period offered our great-grandparents much massive yet finicky furniture such as ebonised cabinets

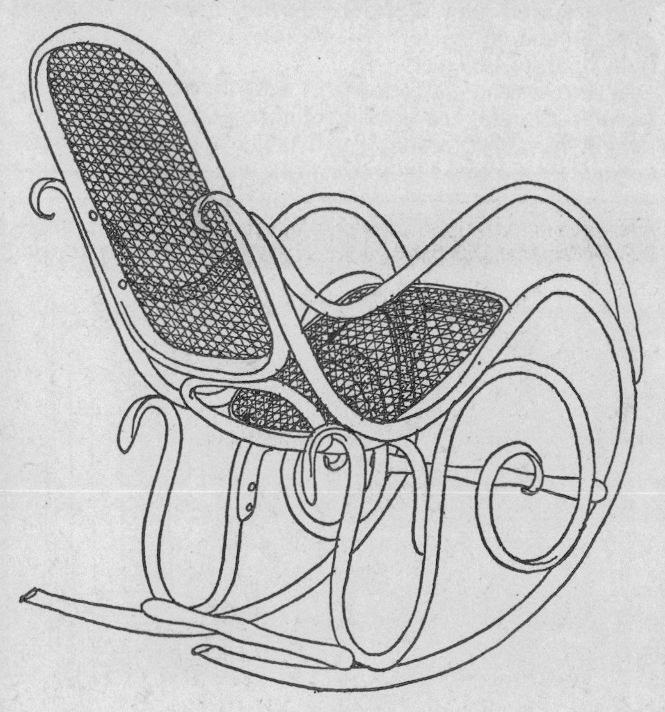

with marquetry grotesques between expanses of bevelled mirror glass among small cupboards and shelves edged with tiny spindles. Japanese arts were discovered and inspired much use of bamboo. Curiously shaped and fretted display furniture was called Anglo-Japanese in catalogues that reflected current demand for novelty with terms like "aesthetic" and "quaint". Less costly pieces such as bedroom suites looked pompous and wasted space with heavy pediments and pedestals.

1900: turn of the century. Dull furniture was made commercially in quantity but collectors find intriguing acknowledgement of continental Art Nouveau. This included elongated, pinched-looking shapes with extended legs and low stretchers and squirming flower ornament. Austere outlines and lively decoration came from a minority of individualistic designers.

Where carving is found this may be amateur work, perhaps including the lettering of mottoes popular on shop-bought furniture. Stools, small tables and cabinets were amateur ornamented by poker work on simple whitewood.

Heavily carved late Victorian cabinet contrasts with striking end of century chair by Charles Rennie Mackintosh.

2. PORCELAIN

England's first porcelain. Milk and honey – symbols of health, wealth and happiness – are represented charmingly on some of England's earliest porcelain, the goat and bee jugs made by the factory at Chelsea. A pair of drowsy goats lie head to tail supporting a jug with a rustic handle and relief decoration of flowers and a magnificent bee. Other vessels were shaped as leaves or shells or patterned in relief with prunus sprays.

This is typical of England's approach to porcelain, inspired by silverware to give a touch of flowery fantasy to useful wares that could at last attempt to challenge the gleaming porcelains of China. Such pioneer English work was produced from the 1740s: by the early 1750s, well to do sophisticates could enjoy the porcelain of at least six rival English factories.

These were the firms whose famous names are the pride of our museums, their work smooth-glazed, translucent, fashionably ornamental – but only a little less fragile than contemporary decorative earthenware.

A porcelain paste held against the light shows one's

Below: early Chelsea scent bottle and goat-and-bee jug; Bow figure. Right: rich coloured Worcester coffee and tea pots.

fingers darkly through its translucent texture: that to most of us is the essential difference between porcelain and generally opaque earthenware. The secret of how to make the hard glossy porcelain of China long remained in the orient, and shipments to Europe were avidly collected by the well to do.

At Meissen, near Dresden, from about 1708, potters used the Chinese ingredients, blending and shaping the paste, covering the vessels in glaze and firing them in an intensely hot kiln so that when they emerged, they were hard, glossy and translucent. Blue ornament could be painted under the glaze, but most other colours were added over it, being fixed by a gentler heat.

This, it must be stressed, was porcelain as the Chinese knew it. England in the 1740s to 1750s – and France too – accepted instead an imitation, making their clay paste translucent by mixing glass ingredients (frit) and firing it before and after glazing. Hence the name frit porcelain and soft paste porcelain to distinguish this imitation from the hard paste porcelain of China.

Chelsea's changing moods. Mellow, soft paste porcelain with a creamy glaze is found in tablewares, ornaments and engaging small personal items such as figure scent bottles. Chelsea, especially, is renowned for these. This pioneer factory was in production from about 1745, marking early wares with an incised triangle. Subsequently anchor marks were used – c. 1749 to 1752, a "raised" anchor on a moulded pad; 1752 to 1756, a very tiny red anchor and 1758 to 1769, a tiny gold anchor.

All these marks have been faked on other porcelain, but museums offer a chance to see real Chelsea porcelain, to enjoy the restrained beauty through the middle period and the colourful gilded magnificence that followed.

Chelsea hen and chickens tureen, 1755. Early works from this factory were of soft paste porcelain with a creamy glaze.

Bow, Derby, Worcester and their rivals. Chelsea's early all white porcelain figures contrast strikingly with later flower decked groups. An early rival of similar charm was Bow, though again the exact starting date is unknown. With Chinese imports in mind, the factory from 1749 was called New Canton and the name is found on souvenir inkwells. This firm, too, was famed for finely painted tablewares including the "Chinese" pattern of two plump partridges and for flowery costumed figures, often raised on high scrolling pedestals.

An important rival to these firms was Derby, from about 1749. Derby came to the fore from 1756 with William Duesbury in control, using a soft paste porcelain with a thick white glaze for figures, ornaments and tablewares.

Most elusive of these early factories was Longton Hall, Staffordshire, at work through the 1750s making tea, coffee and dessert services, flowery candlesticks and vases, elaborate figures and simple pieces such as pickle dishes shaped as leaves and mugs with handles in fanciful loops.

Bristol, about 1749 to 1752, had a factory making table

Below: Bow "New Canton" souvenir inkwell; Bristol soft paste sauceboat, blue underglaze. Right: Longton Hall leaf dish.

wares and rare figures in soft paste porcelain, not to be confused with its later, better known hard paste.

At Bristol one glimpses how mid-18th century potters struggled to strengthen their fine-looking wares. Bow pioneered with animal bone as an ingredient. At Bristol and Worcester Cornish steatite was introduced. This "soapstone" porcelain was heavier but made sturdier, heat resistant tablewares.

Worcester used soapstone to such good effect that their teapots are renowned. Here again one can trace the advance of an important firm, beginning about 1751 with well potted domestic wares, neatly painted in blue under the glaze and advancing in the 1760s to more ambitious work in brilliant colours. Fantastic "japan patterns" imitating oriental imports became especially rich and brilliant at Worcester. Delicate line work in gold over magnificent coloured grounds was popular, too, often surrounding exotic birds in landscapes painted on shapely vases, although for some of this work the white porcelain was sent to London china decorators.

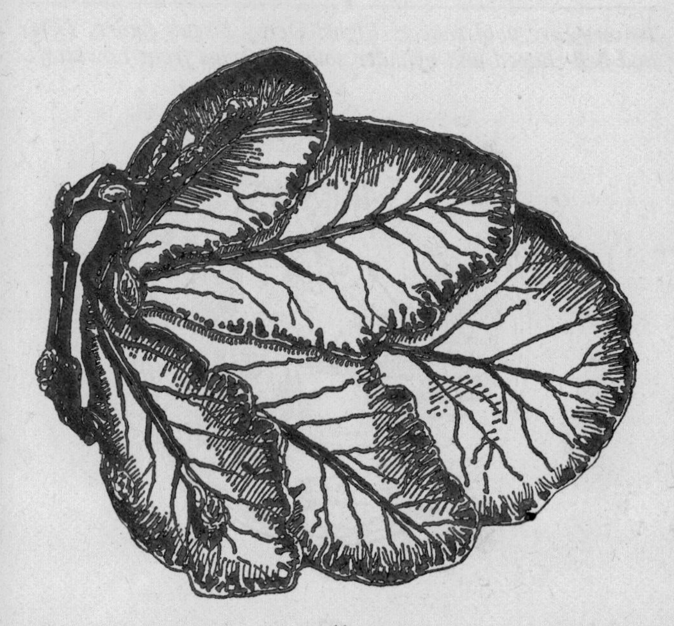

Liverpool and Lowestoft. Worcester served the West Midlands and holiday travellers, including the royal family in 1788 when the firm became the Royal Worcester Porcelain Co. In the north-west, Liverpool had its own potteries, several making soft paste porcelain until late 18th century canals brought a measure of competition from the various Staffordshire potteries.

Chaffers, Christian and Pennington were among leading Liverpool manufacturers in the 1750s to 1760s, some of their soft porcelain containing bone ash or soapstone. Much handsome tableware came from Liverpool, such as punch bowls, punch pots (like teapots but without strainers) and "silver shape" sauce boats. But one-colour ornament quickly printed from transfer papers, which was first used on the porcelain of Bow and Worcester, was successful, too, at Liverpool.

Blue ornament on white is so attractive that we must be thankful that English potters, like the Chinese before them, found it the easiest colour for everyday wares, including transfer printing. Blue could be applied before

---

Below: Liverpool saucer. Right: Derby biscuit figure, 1794, and bell-shaped and cylinder souvenir mugs from Lowestoft.

the glazing but it was found difficult to paint on smoothly.

Lowestoft, like Bow, sprayed it on the ware and, 1757 to c. 1800, met local needs by painting views, even names and birth dates, and making much treasured souvenir wares. Their workaday ware has no association with imported Chinese porcelain painted to commission with heraldic motifs now called "armorial Lowestoft."

Later 18-century splendour. Soft paste porcelain factories continued to contribute important ornaments and tablewares through the later 18th century, inspired still by continental hard paste porcelain, with German Meissen now less favoured than French Sèvres. (French and German porcelain makers tried to stop Bow and Chelsea imports.)

An outstanding artist was William Duesbury, 1725 to 1786, who began as a London porcelain decorator but, with partners, acquired the Derby factory in 1756, Chelsea in 1769, and Bow in 1776. He made Derby porcelain the finest in England, with a restrained grace of design, fine paste and mellow glaze enhanced by well painted ornament like landscapes and botanical specimens. Lavish "Chelsea-

Derby" figures date to 1770 to 1774 when Duesbury controlled the highly skilled Chelsea craftsmen; his talented son (also William) died in 1797.

Another important porcelain maker was engraver Thomas Turner, 1749 to 1809, who left Worcester to establish the Salopian China Manufactory at Caughley (pronounced Calfley) near Broseley, Shropshire, in 1775. There has been much confusion between Worcester's and Caughley's heat resistant, soapstone porcelain tablewares, for example, mask jugs painted and transfer-printed in similar blue patterns, like the charming chinoiserie Fisherman. John Rose of Coalport acquired Caughley in 1799.

At Worcester, too, there were changes. The early Wall-

Below: Worcester tureen, mosaic japan pattern, made c. 1770.
Right: Caughley, Shropshire, cabbage leaf jug, made c. 1775.

Davis period ended in 1783 when Thomas Flight took charge. Magnificent vases were painted and much splendid tableware. Another Worcester decorator, Robert Chamberlain, left the factory in 1783 and with his sons became successful with prestige orders such as armorial dinner services. Thomas Grainger started his own works in Worcester as Grainger Lee and Co. in 1812.

Worcester's georgeous ornament in rich colours and gold contrasts with bisque porcelain, associated especially with Derby in the 1780s and 1790s. Figures in once-fired, soft paste porcelain "biscuit", protected by minimal glazing were sold in-the-white; less perfect pieces were coloured. But far more white figures remain from Victorian days.

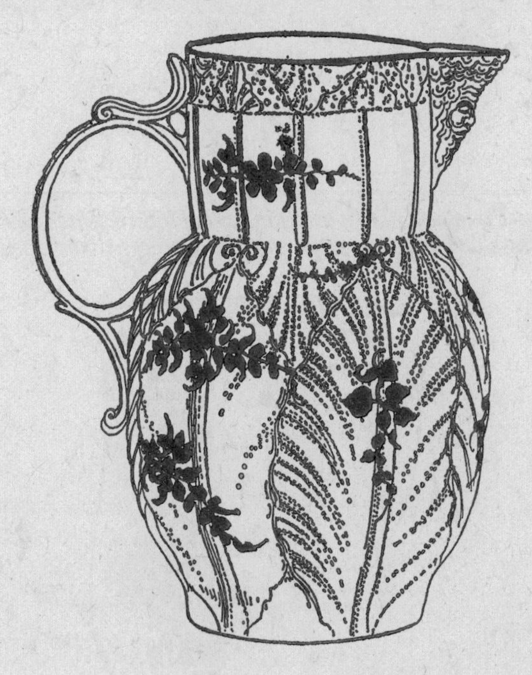

Hard paste porcelain. Some of England's finest hard paste porcelain, too, was left "in the white", including plaques, made only at Bristol, decorated with coats of arms and exquisite little flowers in relief. This venture began at Plymouth in 1768 when Bristol chemist William Cookworthy at last, in Cornwall, found and monopolised the Chinese ingredients of porcelain. In 1770, he moved the enterprise to Bristol.

Heat resistant, hard paste porcelain was well suited to tea ware but much shows the imperfections of a new manufacture and is simply blue-painted under the glaze. In 1773, Richard Champion developed the works more ambitiously, producing figures and ornaments in the Sèvres manner and

Below: Plymouth hard paste tankard, 1768. Right: New Hall straight-sided teapot, 1790, reminiscent of silver fashions.

familiar barrel-shaped teapots. Fashion, alas, preferred to obtain such wares from the Continent and in 1778 he went bankrupt.

He sold his patent to a group of Staffordshire potters who in 1781 launched the New Hall China Manufactory, Shelton. The result is china tableware comparable with the period's silver, such as straight-sided teapots and helmet cream jugs with lively informal ornament – flower sprigs and posies, chinoiseries and landscapes – in the earthenware manner familiar to its founders. Even the porcelain was a compromise, with the English potter's traditional methods of glazing applied to the hard paste.

The practical potters running New Hall accepted further

compromise in 1812, making the form of porcelain known as bone china until about 1835.

The first quarter of the 19th century was a notable period for enterprising English potters of tablewares, for from 1794 continental imports were greatly restricted. Among the finest wares evolved was felspar porcelain made by Josiah Spode II from about 1800 for costly tablewares, brilliantly white and flawless. Coalport made this, too. At Worcester, Chamberlain made his brilliantly translucent Regent china, about 1811 to 1820. But when Worcester firms combined as Chamberlain and Co. in 1840, the world renowned English porcelain was the strong translucent ware we know today as bone china.

World renowned bone china. Bone china is so important that its history is worth recalling. The man responsible was Josiah Spode, 1733 to 1797, an important innovator at his Stoke-on-Trent pottery from 1770. Champion's extended monopoly of the Cornish ingredients for translucent wares ended in 1796. By then Spode was ready to launch his new china, consisting of Cornish hard porcelain ingredients

Below: japan patterned Chamberlain jug, 1799. Right: Spode bone china spill vases, 1810; Grainger openwork vase, 1890.

and of large quantities of calcined, powdered animal bone.

Several other potters were quick to develop this great new enterprise, among the first being Thomas Minton of Stoke, Derby, Coalport, Chamberlain and Grainger of Worcester, John Davenport, and the Herculaneum Pottery at Liverpool. New Hall began in 1812, Wedgwood produced it from 1812 to 1822 and again from 1878.

Josiah Spode's similarly named son and grandson continued the firm until 1829 when control went to W. T. Copeland, whose marks include Copeland and Garrett (1833 to 1847) and others incorporating the name Spode. Before 1820 there were more than 20 makers of bone china. Most ware was unmarked but even when a mark is found it is often no more than a pattern number or title: this meant that a replacement could be ordered only from the china seller who liked to keep his sources secret.

John Rose of Coalport, 1773 to 1828, was an important maker of bone china wares such as delightful flower-encrusted ornaments. Among seldom recorded claims to fame is his invention of a lead-free glaze. Rose's son and

great nephew continued the Coalport pottery through the 19th century, but there are many problems for the Coalport collector.

Much of the early bone china was decorated in London. Towards the mid-century their brilliant bone china imitations of continental work might be given Sèvres or Chelsea marks. The familiar mark Coalport A.D. 1750 (the year claimed for Caughley's start) was introduced in the 1860s when the firm added glazed ornament to many years' accumulation of once-fired "biscuit" china.

Derby was probably making bone china by 1805. Robert Bloor, in command from 1815, is associated with cost-cutting gaudy ornament, but here again there are

Below: heavily ornamented Bloor Derby flower bouquet, 1825.
Right: Davenport teaware, Derby-type japan pattern, c, 1880.

problems for he, too, used up old stocks of china, including late 18th century soft paste porcelain. The works closed in 1848 but were soon reopened, the most important proprietor being Sampson Hancock. Fine bone china was made by the Derby Crown Porcelain Co., established 1876, becoming "Royal Crown Derby" in 1890.

When John Davenport died in 1836 he had 1,400 employees and a thriving export trade in high quality bone china lavishly gilded. Another prosperous china seller, Miles Mason, made china from c. 1800 after the high import tariff of 1794 cut off continental supplies. But he retired – rich – in 1813, his wares overshadowed by his sons' famous "patent ironstone china", a fine earthenware.

Traditional brilliance. The gay glitter of this thriving trade in upstart bone china prompted new efforts from the traditionalists to fashion England's long-loved soft paste porcelains into more exotic wares. Wealthy collectors from the Regency and late Georgian periods sought especially the "old Sèvres" French soft paste porcelain, rarer than the usual hard paste Sèvres.

This involved indirectly two remarkable men, William Billingsley, 1758 to 1828, and Thomas Randall, 1786 to 1859. Billingsley is associated with exquisitely soft-textured flowers painted on other firms' porcelains but his goal was to make his own porcelain as perfect as early Sèvres. With great skill but too little capital he tried again and again, at

---

Below: Billingsley scene on Pinxton, Derbyshire jug, 1800. Right: richly gilded japan pattern on a Swansea dish, 1814.

Pinxton, Brampton-in-Torksey, Swansea and Nantgarw, ending, still dissatisfied, as a decorator at Coalport.

Billingsley's porcelain was too difficult to make as an economical proposition but some superb pieces remain. His friend Randall worked in London decorating porcelain for the china seller Mortlock. But in about 1825 he established himself at Madeley near Coalport, receiving poorly decorated Sèvres porcelain and transforming it into the lavishly coloured and gilded soft paste porcelain, but scarcely any Madeley work was marked.

Randall brilliantly imitated Sèvres coloured grounds, Watteau-esque scenes, chinoiseries and gilding but refused to add Sèvres marks.

Rockingham. Billingsley's first concern was the white porcelain itself; Randall sought merely a porcelain paste worthy of his ornament. Less perfect than Nantgarw, less exotic than Randall-Sèvres, the luxury ware we now associate with the 1820s and 1830s is the bone china produced c. 1826 to 1841, by the Yorkshire pottery known as Rockingham. Patronised by Earl Fitzwilliam, the Brameld brothers indulged in hopelessly costly extravagance: one dinner service cost William IV £5,000 and still proved unprofitable. Now, any piece with the famous griffin mark is treasured, such as the coronet-finished teapot or flower-encrusted scent bottle. But collectors no longer accept most of the period's unmarked flamboyant ornament long attributed to the firm.

Rediscovering Minton. Through research among old pattern books much unmarked ware, long attributed to Rockingham or Coalport, has been recognised as Minton work and it has been possible to date, for example, the changing shapes and patterns of early teaware. As yet, however, the firm seldom gains credit for any of its flower-encrusted

---

Below: lavish Rockingham bone china teapot. Right: Minton flower-encrusted ornament, c. 1830; Alcock classical vase.

ornaments, or its figures, including some in the white that may be misnamed Derby bisque. This important firm – Mintons from 1872 – was launched by Thomas Minton, 1765 to 1836. He was followed by his son Herbert, 1792 to 1858, making bone china, hard paste porcelain, parian statuary and experimental earthenwares. Impressed yearly date symbols were introduced in 1842.

Notable lesser-known firms. Minton was a keen rival to Spode-Copeland but these giants had many other competitors. The Ridgways of Shelton, for instance, made extremely sturdy bone china, often proudly marked with the royal arms and JR & Co.: these included cabinet ornaments as well as colourful tablewares.

The florid style loved by Victorians and too often attributed to Rockingham may often be the work of S. Alcock, active 1828 to 1859, or of G. F. Bowers, who made many a set of "rustic" teapot, cream jug, sugar pot and the rest with handles shaped as branches and feet as sprawling rococo scrolls. But Alcock was among the early Victorian potters who produced wares to meet another mood of his

customers – the utterly different interest in classical art.

Many ornaments remain from this period, finely shaped in formal vase and urn designs and frequently described as Etruscan. But natural flower shapes predominated, none lovelier than those made at Belleek, Co. Fermanagh, from the 1850s. Flowers in full relief might trail over baskets and covered bowls of delicate lattice work, but the major Belleek ornament was marine life. This was suggested by the use of a white matt-surfaced porcelain paste partly covered by a pearly iridescent glaze. Tablewares could be made of extreme thinness because exceptionally pure porcelain materials were locally available. Less fragile wares were evolved in the 1880s.

Below: marine life teapot in pearly glaze Belleek, 1869. Right: Japanese lady in ivory porcelain, Worcester, 1873.

Other intriguing Victorian porcelains. W. H. Goss of Stoke-upon-Trent from 1858 made paper-thin teaware with paste and glaze closely resembling Belleek, but he is remembered especially for some of the other minor porcelain notions that appealed to innovation-loving Victorians, such as his flower jewellery from 1872 – brooches, earrings, and so on, pure white or naturalistically tinted. He also made successful jewelled porcelain. Goss heraldic china was his son's end-of-century creation.

Parian porcelain, basis of Belleek and Goss wares, was the most important early Victorian introduction, much used from 1842 by Copeland, Minton and other major potters. This felspar porcelain, ivory white with a delicate

surface bloom suggesting parian marble, was extremely popular for small statuary. Subjects ranged from classical figures to royalty portraits and sentimental children posed with their pets.

Important artists made the original models and the moulds could produce any number of copies. Some were distributed as minor prizes among subscribers to the Art-Union lotteries held annually in London and some provincial cities, as marks sometimes indicate. Such work is often mistaken for individually sculptured marble. A cheaper form of parian porcelain made ornamental domestic ware such as white jugs decorated in deep relief with story themes.

Most of us share a little of the Victorians' eagerness to marvel. Porcelain lace for a Victorian figure of Ophelia, say, or Cleopatra, is exquisite nonsense associated with Minton, Grainger and others, using an old Rouen technique. Machine-made lace was soaked in cream-like porcelain slip and burned away when the ornament was fired, leaving its pattern in the ware.

Another small continental marvel was the lithophane,

Below: Minton parian dancer, 1849; Copeland parian jug, 1853.
Right: Grainger pâte-sur-pâte – creamy slip on dark paste.

made by such English firms as Grainger. This is usually a plaque of glassy porcelain, its back irregularly surfaced so that when held against the light the hollows and bumps reveal a light and shade picture. Lampshades and nightlight shelters were made with lithophane bases.

From the 1870s, Victorians paid highly for another form of parian ornament made by several potters – pâte-sur-pâte, a wet creamy slip of the porcelain paste applied as decoration on the unfired dark-tinted paste of plaque or vase or pilgrim bottle. Although translucent when thin, as layer after layer was added and dried the whiteness intensified. Delicate tooling completed the cameo effect before glazing and firing. Each piece made in this way was of course unique.

Worcester notably contributed to the vogue for Japanese design, using fine ivory-tinted porcelain softly glazed and decorated in gold and bronze.

Makers' marks. Symbols used by leading 18th century makers are interesting but often appear on fakes and imitations, old and new. But 19th century marks may help,

especially with dating. Worcester, Minton and Wedgwood were among leading firms who used date symbols that changed every year. Many more firms registered their patterns to protect them from copyists: here the familiar mark is a diamond with R^d in the middle, used 1842 to 1883. Figures and letters at the points can be deciphered to tell the date of registration and the Patent Office in London can look up the maker. From 1884 a plain registered number was used, 20th century numbers beginning from 351202.

The words Trade Mark date a piece as no earlier than 1862; England no earlier than 1891, with Made in England as this century's variant.

Many marks give no more than pattern names but sometimes tiny initials are given, too. Really misleading marks include pattern names such as Dresden or Kang-Hsi. Several firms in Victorian days, including the Mortlock china retailers, marked their wares with the 18th century dates claimed for their establishment – and have disappointed beginner collectors ever since.

Porcelain marks: Chelsea-Derby, 1770–1784; Plymouth, 1768–1770; Worcester, c. 1755–1783; Derby, c. 1782–1820.

3. POTTERY

Fragments of pottery are among the earliest traces of ancient civilisations. In contrast to translucent porcelains, my concern is with all other ceramic wares, usually recognised at a glance by being opaque. Collectors distinguish between the most easily kiln-fired earthenwares, porous to liquids until covered with glaze, and the stonewares which were heated until their ingredients become extremely hard and water-tight.

Medieval Britain has left us treasured pieces of brownish earthenwares but we can find all too many brightly gleaming, time-defiant fragments to remind us how earthenwares developed in Georgian and Victorian days as slip-ware, delftware, creamware, lustreware, Prattware. The early

---

Below: slip decorated charger by Thomas Toft, later 17th c. Right: medieval jug with animal spout and 14th c. mask jug.

stonewares – brown, buff, red, black, white – were the forerunners of such delicacies as Wedgwood jasperware.

Early potters shaped their clay vessels and made them watertight by dusting with powdered lead before baking in primitive ovens. Under the resultant yellowish glaze local clays baked to a range of colours – reds, greys, buff, cream – and this prompted the splendidly uninhibited ornament on early slipware plates, posset pots, two-handled tygs and puzzle jugs. Patterns in contrasting colours were created by pressing strips or pads of clay on to the surface or by thinning the clay to the semi-fluid condition called slip and trailing this in bold freehand designs. Some patterns were incised through the slip.

English delftware. Primitive slipware still flourished in Victorian days but, by the late 17th century, fashion wanted Chinese white porcelain decorated in blue, and English potters followed the Netherlands with English delftware. The craft was introduced to London as early as 1570. In the 17th century it became important in Southwark and Lambeth and later Bristol, Liverpool and elsewhere. It was immensely attractive because the coarse, buff-coloured earthenware was wholly hidden by a substantial smooth white covering opacified with costly tin. Naïve freehand ornament was painted on this, ranging from portraits of royalty to chinoiserie; the glaze remained clear of slipware's yellow tinge.

Below: delftware Bristol charger, Lambeth posset pot. Right: stoneware red tea or punch pot, carved Nottingham ware mug.

Handsome stonewares. For workaday use, however, the potter wanted stronger wares, so he forced up the heat of his kilns until the earthy clay-sand mixture hardened into stoneware. Brown stoneware – drainpipe ware to many – has never gone out of use and was adored by aesthetic Victorians. Salt shovelled into the immensely hot kiln gave the ware a rough glaze.

John Dwight founded his long-lived Fulham stoneware factory in 1671, making brown, white, red and a very attractive mottled "agate" stoneware. Unglazed red stoneware is associated with the Elers brothers who came from Holland in 1658, setting a high standard for red teapots, lathe-trimmed and ornamented with motifs "sprigged" to

the surface before firing. Red stoneware, too, continued through the 18th and 19th centuries, made by Wedgwood (rosso antico), Wood, Spode and Hollins, among others.

Throughout the 18th century a wonderfully richly glowing brown with metallic glint was known as Nottingham ware and associated especially with the Morley family, its surface enriched with an iron oxide slip. Some fine Morley vessels show patterns cut through the clay.

The 18th century's common black stoneware, known as Egyptian black, was less important to collectors than improved black basaltes. Far more exciting to the early Georgians was white stoneware. John Astbury, 1686 to 1743, was perhaps the first potter to whiten his clay with crushed burnt flints; this gave him a creamy earthenware, but when fired at a higher temperature the white stoneware could almost pass for porcelain. It was difficult to throw on the wheel, but was mould-shaped in the bold fantastic patterns of early 18th-century silver.

Colour, at first, from the 1720s, was limited to blue-stained, powdered glass sprinkled into incisions before

---

Below: Adam and Eve pew group; Enoch Booth salt-glazed mug. Right: stoneware (crabstock style) and agate ware teapots.

firing. Full colour enamel painting, like porcelain, followed from about 1750. Early Georgian earthenwares were still coarse and fragile but among the most interesting were reddish ware decorated with white raised motifs and glossy black jetware, sometimes gold enriched, associated with Jackfield, Shropshire, from 1751.

Early figures. The 18th century saw spectacular developments in porcelain figure ornaments, but earthenware figures have special appeal. By about the 1730s to 1740s, a few potters were beginning to shape little figures by finger rolling and cutting their clay and dabbing in details like beady eyes and coat buttons with coloured slips. John Astbury may possibly be credited with some early "pew groups". These have no religious significance but the homely men and women are supported by high-backed settles. Other figures in stoneware and earthenware were shaped in simple moulds. Today these precious primitives are usually museum specimens – or the inevitable fakes.

The Astbury family remains elusive, but Thomas Whieldon, 1719 to 1795, can be seen as an immensely important

personality in the story of English pottery. All variegated (tortoiseshell and marbled) wares of his period and later tend to be known as Whieldon wares, although made by Leeds, Liverpool and other Staffordshire potters. These attractive earthenwares were coloured with metallic oxides that flowed and mingled in irregular streaks and blotches in the clear lead glaze.

Whieldon was in partnership with Josiah Wedgwood from 1754 to 1759 and among his apprentices was Josiah Spode. With Wedgwood he developed green-glazed and yellow-glazed wares and the green-and-creamy-yellow effects exploited in pots shaped as cauliflowers or moulded to suggest pineapple or sweetcorn.

Welcome tablewares. World-famous Josiah Wedgwood, 1730 to 1795, benevolent, autocratic industrialist, dominated the Staffordshire potteries. Among his earliest successes was his cream-coloured tableware, a refined earthenware dipped in liquid glaze. This was such a notable improvement that in 1765 Queen Charlotte allowed him to call it queen's ware.

As might be expected, Wedgwood was alert to the

Below: Wedgwood cauliflower teapot; Staffordshire creamware chestnut bowl. Right: Wedgwood creamware centrepiece.

porcelain men's new notion of ornament quickly applied in great detail with paper transfers inked by etched copper plates. Much of his early creamware was sent to Sadler and Green of Liverpool, who were specialists in such one-colour printing from 1756.

Creamware was the first really pleasant everyday tableware and was potted throughout Britain from Staffordshire to Scotland, from Sunderland to Bristol and South Wales. Some especially fine work came from Leeds Pottery who made, catalogued and successfully exported many tablewares that were very light in weight, with a glassy glaze. A number of these examples were painted in enamel colours in the same way as porcelain; other pieces were colour-glazed or transfer-printed or delicately pierced with hand-punches.

Much was left plain but with appealing design detail such as double-twisted and crabstock (crab-apple branch) handles. Elsewhere in Yorkshire the firm was closely associated with Swinton pottery, later famous for Rockingham china, with the Don pottery and with Castleford

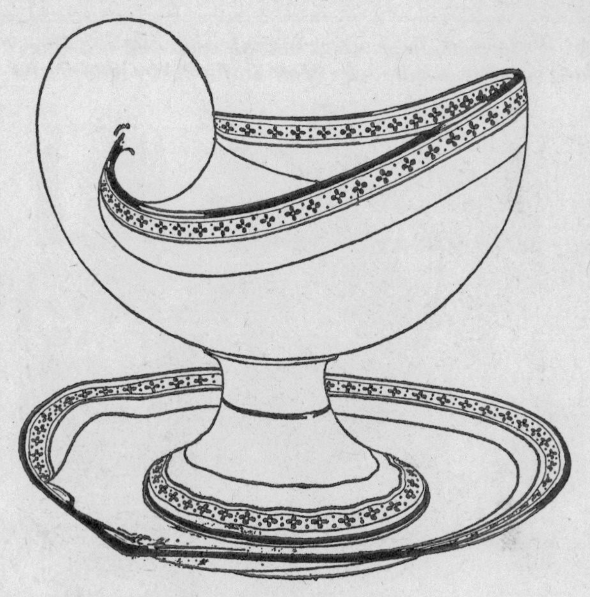

– all of which places were sources, too, of stoneware.

Josiah Wedgwood was debarred by a bitterly contested monopoly from making "true" porcelain, but experimented endlessly to make really white pottery and in 1779 he produced important white pearlware.

To most of us, "Staffordshire blue" means useful wares richly covered with detailed pictures and borders in cobalt blue. Josiah Spode I, 1733 to 1797, and his son were leaders in this underglaze transfer-printing. So clear were these printed patterns that the period could indulge to the full in its adored picturesque views and romantic buildings, in its liking for story scenes and such imagined chinoiserie as the undying willow pattern.

Below: Wedgwood Greek vases: marble mottling, red figures on black basaltes. Right: John Meir Staffordshire blue platter.

Wedgwood blue jasperware. Wedgwood and his partner Bentley (d. 1780) issued finely proportioned earthenware ornaments, too, in neo-classic shapes such as vase and urn, table lamp and inkstand. Some were colour-glazed to suggest marble or porphyry. But he is remembered especially for his velvety, matt-surfaced, fine stonewares. These required no glaze and permitted the quality of detail that he admired in Greco-Roman gem carving for making his ever-popular portrait cameos and decorative bas reliefs in the neo-classic manner.

To most of us Wedgwood means that delicate pale blue jasperware, evolved c. 1774 and still in production, its matt surface patterned with low relief figures that were

mould-shaped separately in white jasperware and sprigged on before firing. From 1785 the white jasper might be coloured merely on the surface (jasper dip) in the restrained, muted colours which we associate with this extremely hard stoneware.

Collectors look not only for the usual range of vessels but for the bas relief panels inserted in chimneypiece and cabinet in the Adam fashion. Wedgwood commissioned leading designers such as John Flaxman RA and scenes from Lady Templetown and Lady Di Beauclerk.

Black basaltes (the modern ware is called basalt) was Wedgwood's improvement from the 1760s on the period's common black stoneware. It was twice-fired to a fine

Below: Wedgwood engine-turned black basaltes teapot, 1778.
Right: jasperware vase by Turner, Lane End, Staffs, c. 1780.

glowing black and used for fashionable busts, bas relief plaques and sets of small medallions. Subjects extended from classical statesmen and writers to modern heroes. So fine was the basaltes' surface that it could be engraved mechanically in the delicate symmetrical line patterns known as engine-turning.

The creamy buff fine stoneware known as caneware was exploited in vessels shaped to suggest strips of bamboo lashed with cane. Caneware vessels realistically shaped as appetising pastry pies were popular, too, around the turn of the century when flour was in short supply.

In all his fine stonewares Wedgwood had a number of rivals: Adams, Turner, Mayer and Neale, for example.

Wood figures and Toby jugs. In the late 18th century the not so rich indulged happily in endless "shams" to suggest wealth and grandeur – not only Sheffield plate and pinchbeck, but splendid pottery figures to mimic exquisite porcelain. Ralph Wood, 1715 to 1772, and his son of the same name, 1748 to 1795, marked some work and so can be linked with the development of figures including such characteristic jugs as the Toby. Related Aaron Wood and his son Enoch, 1759 to 1840, were also important, Enoch being a fine modeller of large vivid portrait figures. The Wood "Vicar and Moses" group was still being reproduced in the early 1960s.

The important colour change in the later 18th-century

Below: Ralph Wood I Toby jug, "The Squire". Right: "Umbrella Courtship", early 19th c.; Pratt moulded jug, 1790s.

figures was from Whieldon-type mingled colours to controlled brush-applied colour glazes and then to the porcelain maker's overglaze painted enamels. Some coarse, unsmiling faces are attributed to the efficient but wayward modeller John Voyez. Voyez signed one familiar jug design shaped as lovers at a tree stump. This type of earthenware moulded with figures in deep relief was extremely popular from about the 1790s and included plaques and jugs.

Projecting ornament especially needed glaze applied over the colours: so-called Prattware was decorated entirely in the limited range of "high temperature" underglaze colours – blue, yellow, purple, brownish-orange and red.

Cottage colour. By then, of course, there was colour in plenty for the earthenware collector, none more appealing today than the everyday wares thickly covered with iridescent metallic lustres. Strangely, although this ware was a new process, far simpler than early Hispano-Moresque lustres, and was made by innumerable early 19th century English potters, it is seldom marked.

Oily solutions of metallic salts were thinly washed over the wares, appearing as bright guinea gold or a deeper gold or silver on pinkish purple. Dark red earthenware gave the gold a coppery tone; pinkish shades came from gold and tin; silver from untarnishing platinum, darkened by adding manganese.

Wedgwood made quantities of a rather blotchy moonlight lustre. Sometimes the ware was entirely covered with lustre to suggest a somewhat clumsy vessel of silver or gold, even to the beaded rims. But more often the potter left reserves for painted decoration. So-called resist lustre was patterned with a substance to repel the metallic solution, which was a background only where there was no

Below: brown Rockingham Cadogan teapot (no lid opening); silver resist lustre jug. Right: silver lustre coffee pot, 1825.

resist. Another type was called Sunderland, although it was also made elsewhere. This covered the ware with a bubbled, splashed effect in purplish or reddish gold and can be found on jugs printed with views of Sunderland's Wearmouth Bridge and simple gift pottery like frog mugs and "framed" text plaques.

The streaky chocolate brown glaze with a wonderful sheen was also popular for cottagey wares far into the 19th century. It was made throughout England and Scotland but is known as Rockingham glaze and is linked with that pottery. The lead glaze was mixed with manganese oxide to a lustrous purple brown and applied thickly by repeated dippings to red earthware vessels such as pots and Toby jugs. The so-called Cadogan teapot may be found, said to be derived from a Chinese wine pot. This lacks a lid opening, being filled through a spiralling tube in the base. Glossy black jetware was popular, and black fireclay ware for massive wine coolers and conservatory urns.

Tea became cheaper and teapots more varied in the early 19th century. The Castleford white stoneware teapot is

interesting, being characterised by vertical ribs between slightly concave panels containing moulded reliefs and a vertical collar around the lid.

Felspathic stonewares, fired at a very high temperature and strong and heat-retaining, became widely important. Castleford was just one of the firms that met the need for stronger domestic wares with "stone china", "new stone", "semi-porcelain", "Saxon stone" and the like, made and marked by Adams, Spode, Davenport, Meigh and others. William Ridgway, among many others, issued notable white stoneware jugs with boldly moulded figure scenes, comparable with Victorian parian ware jugs.

In contrast, the Mason firm lavished colourful, confused

Below: Castleford teapot, moulded relief, blue stripes, 1800. Right: japan patterned vase in Mason's patent ironstone.

"japan" patterns on their hard white earthenware which was called patent ironstone china: their most popular articles ranged from the familiar sets of octagonal jugs to Victorian fireplaces.

Lava ware was another heavy and strong cottage ware. Collectors of once-cheap white wares delight in the mug which contains a frog climbing up the inside towards the drinker's mouth.

Another cheap underglaze decoration consists of fine, wavering lines suggesting ferns or moss, and known as mocha. Any factory child would be able to turn and twist the vessel while a blob of acid-based colour diffused through a band of wet clay slip.

Figures and flatbacks. Coarse brown stoneware was still in demand, too, for workaday Derbyshire hunting jugs and for the simple spirit flasks by Doulton and other firms, topped by head-and-shoulders busts intended for pub use, often as propaganda, from about the 1820s to 1840s.

But for chimney shelf in villa and well-furnished cottage the early 19th century offered far more colourful ornaments. Guileless figures cheaply potted in brittle earthenware provided endless reminders of long-loved biblical stories. They offered homesick recruits to the factory towns gleams of the sentiment, humour and even the animals of their childhood.

John Walton, at work c. 1806 to 1835, gave his figures

Below: John Walton sheep against a bocage background, 1825.
Right: Obadiah Sherratt group of Polito's menagerie, 1814.

crude little bocage backgrounds of oak leaves. His work might be impressed WALTON but this may also be found on reproductions. Ralph Salt, 1782 to 1846, made figures in a similar style, as did Thomas Rathbone of Portobello, Edinburgh, c. 1808 to 1850. Among others, Obadiah Sherratt, 1776 to 1840s, produced ambitious groups often with a streak of robust humour. Typically, the marbled base had four feet linked with a wavy frieze. Many other splendid little figures came from Sunderland, including some of the spotted lustre dogs loved by early Victorians.

By the 1840s, however, the vogue had begun for flat-backs. For cheapness the figure was often shaped in a single, somewhat tapering mould, the back left plain, the

front quickly hand painted. Innumerable named "portraits" sold mainly on their topicality. Colour details such as royalty's ermine dots might aid recognition, but as the body became white, brilliantly glazed, colour became minimal. Bright liquid gold was first used in 1853, but the collector can date most specimens by subject or dress – and must be wary of reproductions.

A similar naïve commentary on passing events delights the collector of picture pot lids, but here the process was a highly sophisticated development of full colour transfer printing, evolved by Jesse Austin, 1806 to 1879, working for F. and R. Pratt. Pots of hair pomades, fish pastes and the like had slightly rounded lids after 1848.

Pot lid pictures followed current taste with story-telling themes, but critics bewailed the gulf between art and industrial ornament, shown for example by the 1851 Great Exhibition. Talented, well-intentioned artists would paint inappropriate pictures on vase and pilgrim bottle and designers knew little of craft techniques.

Herbert Minton, however, won wide success from 1848

Below: Pratt paste pot. Right: Minton Henri Deux tazza, 1878, and Palissy ewer, 1869; Doulton silicon ware vase, 1888.

by employing Léon Arnoux, 1816 to 1902, French chemist, potter and eventually art director. Among successes were majolica, Palissy ware and Henri Deux inlaid pottery. His majolica, widely imitated, was mould-shaped in deep relief ornament and covered with rich color glazes. Articles ranged from fireplaces to ladies' workbaskets, from figures to cheese stands.

Victorian art pottery. Minton's was one of the few firms using impressed yearly date symbols. But the later 19th century's more interesting work dates itself by its fascinating reflection of the strengths and limitations of the new craft-conscious aesthetes.

Doulton of Lambeth produced some early 19th century commemorative stonewares, but was mainly important for domestic and industrial wares until the 1860s when the Lambeth School of Art collaborated in art wares. Hard brown stoneware, from clock cases to chessmen, was variously coloured, incised, stamped and carved before being once-fired – including salt glazing – along with common domestic wares. Silicon stoneware, with a slight

smear glaze, was incised, stamped and patterned with raised slip in the pâte-sur-pâte porcelain manner. Marqueterie ware, imitating Tunbridge marquetry in wood veneers, cut slices from blocks of coloured clays to build decoration.

Some valuable Doulton work is artist signed. Artist designs carried out by students may be marked X. Other Doulton artists painted and gilded pilgrim bottles and the like in fine earthenware called Lambeth faience (more costly Crown Lambeth from 1892).

Terracotta was rediscovered by early Victorians, especially for conservatory ware. This soft earthenware, unglazed and porous, ranged from glowing red to yellow and brown, its slightly glossy surface well suited to painting in the approved ancient Etruscan manner. Ambitious terracotta relief panels, such as biblical scenes, were created at Doultons from 1866 by the modeller George Tinworth, 1843 to 1913.

Also in the London area, the four Martin brothers ran their own studio pottery at Southall, 1877 to 1915, working new wonders with stoneware, including many colours and

---

Below: George Tinworth terracotta relief of Doulton's staff. Right: Martin grotesque vase, 1888; De Morgan lustre dish.

surface textures. It is a pity they are remembered for grotesques like Walter's Wally bird tobacco jars.

Many artist potters were absorbed with metallic oxide lustres. William Morris's friend, William De Morgan, 1839 to 1917, created satisfying two-dimensional patterns in intense metallic lustres and "Persian" blues and greens. Rich colour, and originality in controlling it with incised line patterns, are found in the rather casually finished work of Harold Rathbone, at Birkenhead from 1894. Splendid, streaky, oriental colour glazes fascinated many studio potters in the 1880s to 1890s. At Linthorpe, Bretby, Swadlincote and Burmantofts glaze colours dominated bold, sometimes eccentric oriental and Art Nouveau shapes, some by Christopher Dresser.

In early 20th century work, William Moorcroft is remembered for rich, deep colours subtly blended in fruit and leaf patterns; the Ruskin Pottery, Smethwick, for freckled pink, blue and violet glazes; and Pilkington Tile and Pottery Co. for its "Royal Lancastrian" lustres.

More difficult to date are Victorian traditional country

wares like red earthenware harvest jugs by the Fishley family, Fremington, Devon. More sophisticated slipwares, all too prone to the period's "quaintness", were made at Barnstaple, Clevedon and Aller Vale.

Sussex is associated with nest-egg hen-and-chickens moneypots and the pig divided at the neck into jug and cup. Rye made vessels decorated with separately shaped hop sprays, but more elaborate primitive motifs were attached all about the huge brown barge teapots of the South Derbyshire area. On the intriguing pottery of Castle Hedingham, Essex, 1864 to 1901, these motifs might include 17th century dates.

I have scarcely mentioned pottery tiles. Collectors quickly realise that these perfectly represent the styles and moods of different periods. Minton's were making tiles from the 1830s, but their main Victorian popularity dates from the 1870s, when they were made by Copeland, Wedgwood, Doulton, Maw and Co. and many others. One may still get them direct from the wall or alcove where they were fashionable adornment in theatre, shop and home.

Country wares: puzzle jug, Rogers and Son, Crock Street Pottery, 1864; "Feare God" mug, Castle Hedingham, 1890.

4. *GLASS*

Over 2,000 years ago, when the craft of glassmaking was already 2,000 years old, ancient Syrians shaped hot glass with blowpipes just as glass-blowers make some of our finest table glass today. The Egyptian and Roman empires have left us fascinating glass relics. In Lancashire, the modern glass centre of St. Helens is less than 10 miles from Warrington's Roman occupation factory.

By medieval days the Venetians were expertly fashioning this fragile soda glass and it was a Venetian, Verzelini, who first became successful with such delicate wares here, as glassmaker to Elizabeth I. Little of his Anglo-Venetian work remains, however, and more of today's collectors enjoy the substantial shapes of early English bottles in dark, workaday glass.

World renowned flint glass. England's world renown for table glass developed only after 1674 when George Ravenscroft evolved a new formula and with this was able to make "the finest and noblest glass", then called flint glass and now usually known as lead crystal. This stalwart glass, heavy and shadowy with lead, suited the sturdy

Below: 16th c. Verzelini goblets. Right: Ravenscroft jug, roemer, posset cup, c. 1680; early flint-glass wine glasses.

vessels that were so favoured on English tables. Compared with fragile continental glass, it possessed a wonderful refractive brilliance and a resonant ring.

No new collector wants to be overwhelmed by a long list of technical terms. Briefly, a red hot "gather" of this glass could be inflated by the glassblower into the bowl of what is known as a free-blown glass. As glass, when hot, can be joined without trace, a team of glassmen could attach stem and foot to a drinking glass bowl, leaving no more than a "ponty scar" under the vessel's foot where it was held on the end of an iron pontil rod.

Heat treatment – annealing – toughened the glass (the hollow "kick" under an early decanter aided this) and for strength early foot rims were turned in (welted or folded). These welted feet and ponty scars continued long on country work.

In the early 18th century, drinking glasses still had heavy bowls on thick stems and wide welted feet. The stem might be drawn as a tapering extension of the bowl, sometimes enclosing an air bubble "tear". Or it might be stuck

to the bowl and foot, being shaped in a baluster outline, the Hanoverians' silesian shouldered-pedestal or an arrangement of swellings called knops.

Some other delights of this time include sweetmeat glasses and custard cups arranged on glass salvers. Stemmed salvers – two or three on top of each other – made colourful pyramids for the informal social gathering known as a dessert. Glasses made to hold dry sweetmeats have ornamental rims; vessels for frothy syllabubs are wide-rimmed and narrow-bowled.

A decanter may be found in shaft-and-globe or mallet shape with a ball stopper; or a baluster candlestick on a high moulded foot. But by the 1740s all this was changing.

18th c. decanters. From left: mallet with ball stopper, quatrefoil, wide-shouldered, narrow-shouldered (Williamite).

GLORIOU

Early cut glass. Collectors welcome the change to lighter table glass. The annealing process improved, so that the design could become more delicate and as a glass tax calculated by weight of ingredients was imposed in late 1745, the glassmen had to make the most of their materials. Many collectors think this early Georgian flint-glass tableware of the 1740s to 1770s – light, small scale and delicately ornamented – the loveliest ever made.

By blowing glass into a patterned mould before expanding it fully, it could be given a gently rippled surface, but far more effective patterns were achieved by delicately grinding shallow facets or diamond shapes into the glass– the work of a separate group of craftsmen. Grinding with several different shapes of wheel also produced almost all the line ornament.

Exception to wheel engraving was freehand line work done with a diamond point – rare but never entirely out of use. Beginners sometimes confuse diamond engraving with the term diamond cutting applied to wheel-ground, diamond-shaped patterns. Wheel engraving included

---

Below: four 18th c. engraved wine glasses; enamelled Beilby goblet, 1762. Right: Stuart symbols on Jacobite glasses.

delightful patterns such as the ale glass hop-and-barley. Flowered glasses suggesting porcelain ornament were for the potent cordial served with evening tea.

Jacobite glasses with wheel engraving (mainly from around 1745) commemorate loyalty to the Stuart cause: these are often faked. Some decanters are magnificently engraved with names and flourished "labels."

Colours and gold. Examine an engraved glass very closely and you will see how each flower petal and tendril was laboriously cut with the fine edge of the manually revolved wheel. The obvious alternative was surface ornament, brush applied in enamel or gold. The finest enamel ornament in dense white and colours is attributed to William Beilby of Newcastle and his sister Mary, at work in the 1760s to 1770s – heraldic work, rococo scrolling, even landscapes, sometimes "signed" with a tiny butterfly (and often faked).

Gold rims have often worn off the 18th century glass but gilded ornament is sometimes found on later 18th century vessels. Burnished mercury gilding dates from

the 1780s onwards but glittering gold is found only from about 1855.

Ornament on drinking glass bowls ranged from fruiting vines on long-stemmed champagne flutes to the cider maker's propaganda words "No Excise" on the bucket bowls of cider glasses around 1760. But a special kind of ornament appeared about the mid 18th century. Ancient Rome delighted in this process which filled straight or swelling wine glass stems with spirals of air or white enamel or brilliant colours. The so-called mercury twist consists of thick corkscrew air spirals in especially brilliant glass. Such stems are smooth to the touch but some straight stems, c. 1740s to 1800s, were surface-incised and others, now very valuable, were cut all over on the grinding wheel into concave facets.

Gold ornament was most effective on the clear, coloured glass widely used from the 1750s. Flint glass's own refractive fire was largely lost but lovely effects could be achieved in shades of deep blue, cool watery green and heavy red that was less vermilion bright than the imported red glass

Below: faceted and enamel-twisted stems on drinking glasses. Right: painted opaque white glass, and gilding on Bristol blue.

of Bohemia (Czechoslovakia). Blue nowadays seems always to be called Bristol blue but in the 1760s this was specifically a refined form of cobalt blue from Saxony. The disruption of the Seven Years' War meant that for a time only one Bristol dealer could supply this magnificent colour.

Clear glass decanters were always required for holding wines but the late 18th century has also left us many sets of spire-finialed decanters and squares for spirits in blue glass named in gold. All the smaller table accessories may be found, too, for blue glass splendidly set off stands and perforated casings of silver or Sheffield plate. Smaller bottle shapes were gold-labelled for toilet waters and delicately ornamented for scent.

Opaque white glass was advertised as enamel glass in the 1760s, soft-surfaced and brittle but popular for jugs and sugar basins, candlesticks and vases, enamelled and gilded with flowers, birds and all the gay nonsense of contemporary porcelain. Some was transfer-tinted. A poorer quality from the 1770s shows a fiery opalescence against the light – called in the 19th century sunset glow.

Wide-ranging neo-classic design. This cheaper white ware was a poor, low-taxed lime soda glass, for the tax on flint glass was doubled in 1777. Flint glassmen then found they had to concentrate on high quality work, light in weight, the well-proportioned, gracious designs suiting the neo-classic mood.

Technically, glass continued to improve, although the merest hint of colour remained – either lacking or overdone in many fakes. Slender decanters sloped inward or outward from shoulder to base, perhaps ornamented with wheel engraving, enamelling, gilding or shallow facet-cutting, matched on stoppers with finials shaped as spires or vertical discs or ovals. Often long, shallow flutes decorate the neck and lower body: in the barrel decanter, shallow lines suggest hoops and staves.

Quite as important in contributing sparkle to fashionable apartments was the candlestick, elaborated into the branching candelabrum and spectacular hanging chandelier. Neo-classic silver prompted pillar designs on domed and terraced feet and the vase candlestick with an urn-shaped

---

Below: late 18th c. decanters. Right: urn finial chandelier, c. 1770; vase and facet cut candlesticks, c. 1800 and 1780.

body on a square plinth. Gilded ormolu was combined with flashing cut glass in brilliant candelabra. Two or four curved branches supporting candle sockets extended from a central supporting stem. Pear-shaped drops or lustres and elaborate star finials with sparkling faceted surfaces were in huge demand for candelabra and chandeliers. The period's girandole candlestick is charming, hung with twinkling lustres.

Drinking glasses of the 1770s to 1790s are challengingly varied, the long established wine glasses, champagne flutes and decorative, small-bowled cordials being augmented, for instance, by the massive short-stemmed rummer. The toddy rummer appeared in the late 1780s, a purely English vessel for mixing the popular fireside drink of spiced rum and hot water. This first had an ovoid bowl, thick stem and heavy square foot. By the 1800s, the bowl might be a bucket or barrel shape, always a field for pictorial engraving. A glass pipette, or toddy lifter, transferred the hot rum to glasses.

Dram and firing glasses were made for social occasions,

too. The small spirit dram of the early 18th century with little or no stem and wide foot was developed in the second half of the century into a stumpy glass on a heavy flat disc foot intended for repeated banging on the table as "fire", a form of acclamation.

To keep sober, toastmasters had their own deceptive-bowled glasses. The slender flute sometimes called a ratafia glass was probably intended for the potent brandy drink known as surfeit water.

But the most confusing vessel of this period is the Williamite glass. The glass itself may be late 18th century and the ornament refers to William III (1689 to 1702), but its concern was with end-of-century political controversy and some date from as late as the 1820s (see page 91).

Regency sparkle. Improvements in annealing meant that English flint glass was stronger still by the end of the 18th century, prompting bolder cutting. Much glass was cut with V-shaped wheels into patterns of raised diamond points that the cutters sometimes further notched in what they called cross-cut, hobnail and strawberry detail. Other

Below: cut glass notched diamond patterns. Right: toddy lifter and rummer; early 19th c. Irish kettledrum fruit bowl.

wheels patterned the glass with horizontal, vertical and fan-shaped prismatic cutting or scattered stars and sprigs and the circular concavities called printies. Long icicle lustres became popular at this time, followed by flat-surfaced, hanging prisms.

Decanters, for example, became massive with broad rings of cut glass round their necks to make the weight easier to lift. Stoppers were vertical targets, flat mushrooms or diamond-cut spheres. Wide-shouldered decanters, cylindrical and slightly tapering "Prussian", belong to the early 19th century, some with heavy vertical reeding as body ornament.

Ships' decanters may sometimes be found, too; they are extremely wide-based and narrow-shouldered, so that they would stand steady in a gale.

Some especially heavy glass is often called Waterford, but it is a mistake to think most Irish glass is distinguishable from the English that it sought to copy. For a time it was exempt from tax but even this advantage ended in 1825, when the tax was 10½d. per lb. of flint glass. A very

little was marked by Belfast, Dublin and Cork glasshouses and certain shapes, such as kettledrum and canoe fruit bowls, seem to have been popular with Irish glassmen. There is, too, a pattern of oval and diamond lozenges formed of intersecting circles, found on decanters and the like, usually known as the Cork vesica.

Among all this cut glass glitter, a special delight is the Apsley Pellatt crystal cameo. Here again was a notion that depended upon the perfect fusion of hot glass. A small bas relief portrait, often royalty, was cast in china clay and completely enclosed in particularly clear flint glass. Pellatt made paperweights and other ornaments between 1819 and 1835; these were copied less perfectly around the 1850s.

Apsley Pellatt crystal cameo of George IV. China clay bas relief enclosed in a flint glass paperweight. Early 19th c.

Pressed glass. Brilliant cutting served as a background to Pellatt's silvery cameos, but cutting gradually lost favour after an American process for pressing glass was introduced in the 1830s. A plunger forced the hot glass into a mould and produced vessels that were almost as sharply patterned as those hand cut on the wheel.

The blown-moulded process was improved early in the 19th century but it is easy to distinguish this more gently moulded patterning, felt by the fingertips inside the vessel. In pressed glass the vessel's interior is left smooth by the plunger. Dishes and mugs, bowls and tumblers were all pressed and in the 1870s to 1880s great use was made of stippled grounds and raised dots.

Below: pressed glass jubilee plate with raised dots, 1887.
Right: Nailsea flask, white enamel decoration, early 1800s.

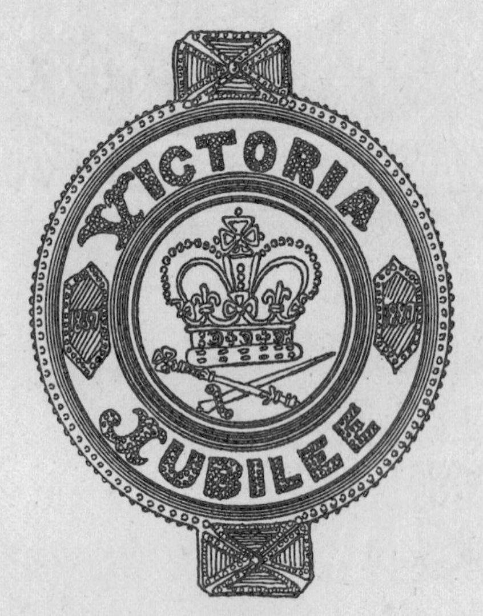

Nailsea pleasures. Pressed glass was a cheap follower of fashion. The glass for working folk was so-called Nailsea and, from the 1790s onwards, this made use of cheaply taxed bottle glass. Simple vessels in the murky glass might be flecked and looped with white or rolled in colourful waste glass chippings. By the 1800s, it was found that the glass could be cleared to pale green, often coloured an opaque dark blue or amber.

Nailsea was a source of superior crown glass, but gave the name to this gay bottle glass work, made at Newcastle, Sunderland, Alloa and elsewhere. Articles ranged from jugs and conjoined gimmel flasks to such imitative nonsense as giant tobacco pipes. Stoppered rolling pins, for instance,

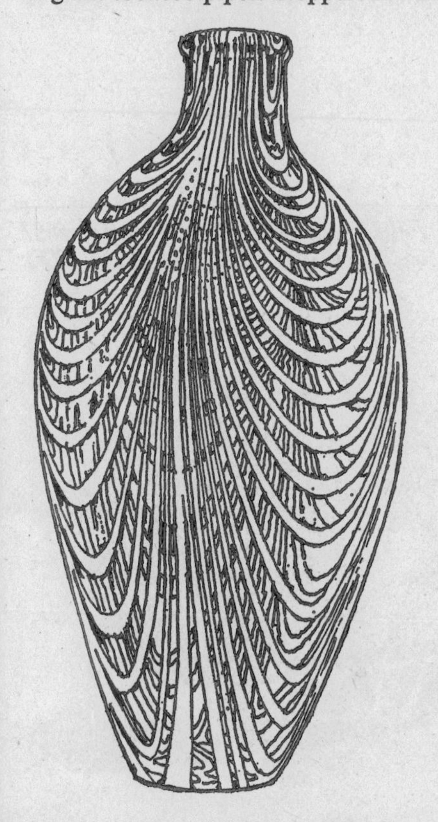

were flecked and streaked at first, but in later years, made in coloured or opaque white glass, they might be painted or transfer-printed with good luck verses.

For centuries, among working folk, spun glass caused shop front or street corner wonderment as a man or woman with rods of glass and a small blow-lamp made a variety of imaginative tiny ornaments.

Doubtless some so-called friggers were spare time creations but far more of this work, such as delicately rigged ships, came in the late 19th century from small commercial ventures that also met the renewed demand for glass walking sticks, hunting horns and other examples of this fascinating craft.

Below: Nailsea-style rolling pin, flecked jug. Right: enamel painted Stourbridge jug, cased ruby glass decanter, c. 1850.

Victorian colour. The year 1845 was enormously important to English glassmen. The heavy tax on flint glass was abolished and at last there was a chance to experiment in flint glass with continental notions where glass made up in colour what it lacked in sparkle. Coloured clear glass became popular and clear glass painted in enamel colours was soon followed by more ambitious cased glass – something you either admire or detest.

You may find cased glass decanters, wine glasses, vases and toilet water bottles. Cased scent bottles include the double-ended type still offering a whiff of aromatic smelling salts at one end and "handkerchief" scent at the other. The clear glass was covered with layers of coloured glass,

often including opaque white. All were perfectly fused together, so that the cutter could slice through to the clear glass, revealing the intervening colours in simple patterns. Layers of clear glass were used, too, to enclose a silver solution or even metallic spangles, for table vessels. Some were lightly ground to suggest frosting, some had the silver covered with clear coloured glass – compared at the time to the sheen of humming bird feathers.

But collectors today value especially the period's millefiori (thousand flowers) paperweights, that were first made in England in the late 1840s. Each flower consisted of a slice cut from a glass rod built up layer upon layer round a central core and then drawn out without disturbing the pattern. When cold, slices from different rods could be arranged on a clear glass base and closely covered with a magnifying glass dome.

Bristol dumps – high-domed door-stops in a coarse green glass – came later in the century and continued to the 1920s, their ornament often no more than a fountain of air bubbles pricked into the hot glass. Mid Victorians

Below: opaline vase; millefiori (thousand flowers) paperweight. Right: goblet engraved with bacchantes, all c. 1850.

also favoured peculiarly lifeless semi-opaque opaline glass. Much of this was painted with massed flowers but the figure scenes were copied from ancient Grecian pottery. Sometimes a plain vessel with typical rounded shaping was contrasted with relief ornament such as the period's adored reptiles.

The vogue for engraving. Tours de force were shown by glass cutters at the 1851 Great Exhibition at Crystal Palace. So sharp and hostile to the fingers was their diamond patterning, to defy the makers of pressed glass, that it comes as no surprise to find Victorians of the 1850s to 1870s preferring yet another alternative – delicate wheel engraving on clear glass.

This dated back to the early 18th century and was carried into the 19th when massive rummers displayed ships, Masonic emblems, even scenes like Wearmouth bridge and the Tyne suspension bridge. All manner of imaginative engraving in intricate, revived rococo and classic fantasy was now approved on decanters, vases in Grecian outlines, tall straight water jugs, loving cups,

carafes and newly fashionable, hemispherical champagne cups. There were flowers and trailing foliage too, and feathers and popular ferns. Mostly this was wheel engraving, but a little was drawn with a diamond point and some was etched with acid, a very much cheaper process.

By the 1880s, cut glass was in vogue again but engravers achieved new success with a glossy style of polished wheel engraving that was known as rock crystal glass. A glass with the sultry beauty of rock crystal had been a triumph of 16th century Venice and it is easy to find Venetian inspiration in most of the novelties that go under the name of fancy glass.

Exhibitions, like the one held in Paris in 1867, reflected

Below: pressed end-of-day glass plate, c. 1870. Right: Stourbridge vases and epergne with hanging vessels, late 19th c.

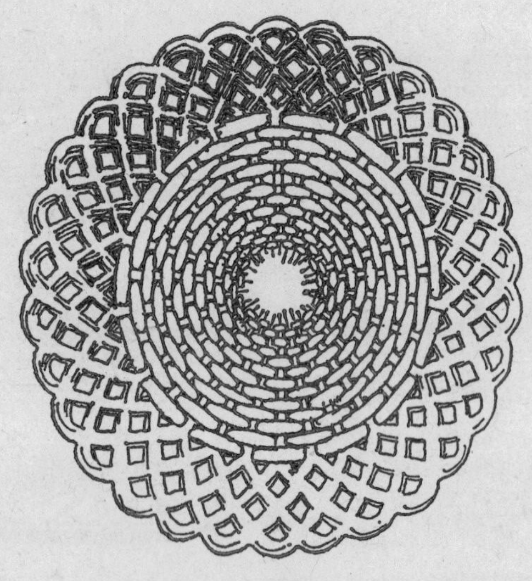

a revivial of interest in early techniques by the Venetians. But English glassmen, advancing from silvered, gilded and frosted glass of the mid-century, could use their own substantial flint glass in place of the more fragile Venetian lime soda glass.

Tableware affected by the new notions included jugs, bowls, drinking glasses, and the popular decanter in inverted egg shape on a narrow foot, the tall, thin neck topped by a rim shaped in three out-curving folds and supporting a long-necked stopper. Flower vases included the epergne where the central vase on a broad plateau base was surrounded by scrolling arms supporting smaller vessels. Among fancy glass the collector chooses her own

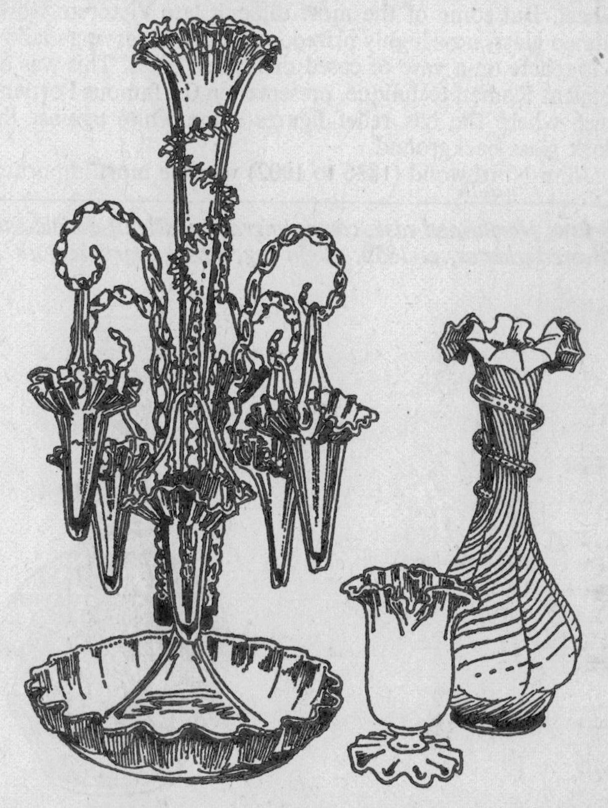

favourites from "crackle ice" to an acid-induced satin finish. Delicate threads of coloured glass might be wound tightly round a vessel's stem or handle. Trails and frillings were in vogue again and sophisticated quilted effects with air bubbles trapped between layers of glass.

Semi-opaque "Burmese" glass of the 1880s was heat-shaded from yellow to deep pink. Opaque marbled glass incorporating steelworks slag was pressed into spill vases, baskets, jugs, sometimes bearing makers' marks and called end-of-day glass.

Cameo glass. In these days of mass production it may be well to stress that all glass cutting and wheel engraving is individual handwork, the glass held against a revolving wheel. But some of the most difficult late Victorian work, cameo glass, now highly prized, consisted of carving shallow bas reliefs on a vase of cased or layered glass. This was an ancient Roman technique, preserved in the famous Portland vase where the bas relief figures show white against the dark glass background.

John Northwood (1836 to 1902) was the most important

Below: Northwood vase, cameo engraving. Right: double-wall silvered glasses, c. 1850; Elgin jug, wheel engraving, 1873.

English exponent and was successful, too, with so-called intaglio engraving where the ornament was hollowed into the glass. George and Thomas Woodall made some fine cameo glass but to ensure commercial success the carving was soon being aided by grinding and acid to remove unwanted background. Some cameo work is marked. By the 1890s, some semblance of this work was achieved with thick white paint. American Mary Gregory figures which were painted in white on clear glass date to the 1870s to 1880s, the childish antics widely copied ever since, often very badly and sometimes with tinted faces.

Another American fashion popular here from late in the century was brilliant-cut glass, with immensely elaborate tiny detail. Nothing unorthodox could be expected of this status symbol work, but even here the tall, attenuated end-of-century outlines dominate the glittering array of tall-stoppered, long-necked decanters, narrow-handled claret jugs, wasted water jugs and champagne jugs with central ice cylinders. The metal tantalus frame would lock away three stoppered vessels without hiding

their grandiose cutting. Even the sugar basin might have a faceted stem on a star-cut foot.

Art Nouveau was expressed in tall, excessively slender drinking glasses and flower flutes. In contrast, the late Victorian enthusiasm for Japanese art meant low, squarish vessels on corner feet. Some examples reflected the fashion for rustic work, such as hollow tree-stump vases that persisted far into Edwardian days.

Glass makers of the 19th century. Important in Britain were the Bacchus, Osler and Richardson firms, Stevens and Williams and Thomas Webb. The Scottish Couper firm made notable clutha glass, full of random bubbles, and in some satisfying shapes by Christopher Dresser.

In France, Rousseau, Gallé and Lalique ranged far and wide among glass techniques, as did Loetz in Austria and Tiffany in America. Among Tiffany's rivals was Englishman Frederick Carder (1863 to 1963), an important designer with Stevens and Williams until he went to America in 1903. Before his retirement, Carder enjoyed another 56 years of brilliant, inventive work.

The influence of Art Nouveau. Wavy line decoration and writhing sunflowers on a tall dark glass vase, c. 1900.

5. *SILVER*

More fortunate than ever today is the child born with a silver spoon – first introduction, perhaps, to a lifetime of silver collecting, far more rewarding, assuredly, than even its ever-increasing monetary value.

From time immemorial man has appreciated this benign metal. One has only to visit ancient mountain workings to realise what he would hazard for such treasure. Its gleaming brightness has complimented his beeswax candles; its purity has preserved the subtlest flavour and proved smooth to his lips in loving cup and wine taster.

But silver has to be hardened for use with a little copper, and silversmiths still submit their wares to testing and marking to maintain ancient rules of quality.

Finely engraved silver beaker, 1690, part of a set including folding knife, fork and spoon for a well-to-do traveller.

Hallmarks. As early as the 14th century, standards of purity for both silver and gold were firmly established in London: the great Worshipful Company of Goldsmiths was incorporated in 1327. The amount of copper alloy that was permitted in sterling silver was defined and a system of testing (known as assaying) and punch-marking was established and so rigorously maintained that anyone today handling a piece of silver plate turns instinctively first to the row of tiny punched "hallmarks," noting the exact details of their features and also the puncheon outline.

Accepting the fact of occasional deliberate deception, these must be considered along with the general style of the piece of silver, the way in which it is made, its design and, of course, any ornament.

When these are "right," the hallmarks fascinatingly fill in the details. They testify to the quality of the metal (the proportion of copper alloy) and show the town where the quality was tested, together with the date, the silversmith and, between 1784 and 1890, the tax paid. The collector usually begins with the date letter, originally included so

---

Marks: Below: London lions; Britannia; lion's head erased, Scottish lion, Irish harp, Hibernia. Right: monarchs' heads.

that faulty testing could be punished. Each assay office in the British Isles used its own series of letters in different founts and within different punch outlines, changing each St. Dunstan's day (30 May).

This system has meant some repetition. A full list of London and provincial date letters in their punch outlines is essential for any collector.

Besides the date letter, one looks for the town mark. Most familiar, perhaps, are London's so-called leopard's head (a full face lion head, crowned until 1821) and, from 1773, Birmingham's anchor and Sheffield's crown. The other usual lion mark is the heraldic lion walking to the left. Until 1821 the head was turned full face. Since then, it has looked straight ahead. On London silver the heraldic lion indicated sterling quality.

Such silver was in short supply for coin, 1697 to 1720, and silversmiths had to use still purer silver marked with a figure of Britannia and a lion's head with a wavy neckline ("erased"). Britannia, or high standard silver, and its marks have been in minor use ever since. Yet another date guide is the

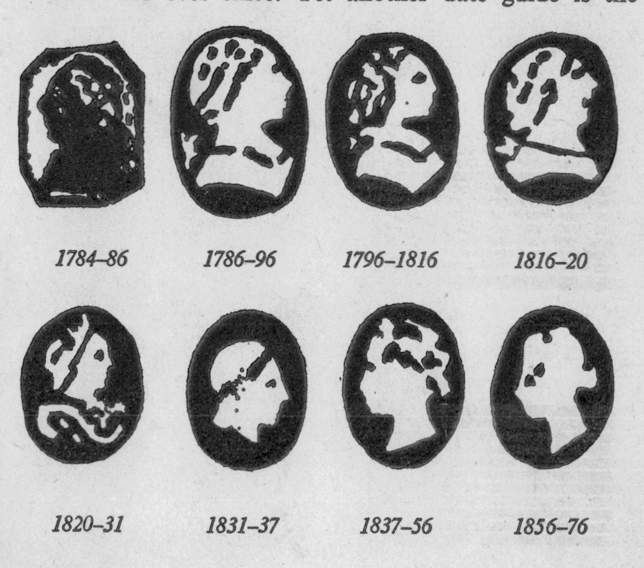

1784–86 *1786–96* *1796–1816* *1816–20*

1820–31 *1831–37* *1837–56* *1856–76*

monarch's head, showing the maker's payment of tax between December 1784 and 1890. Doubled tax in 1797 to 1798 meant two impressions of George III's head on that years' silver.

Makers' marks lost their early symbols in favour of initials (the first two letters of the surname on Britannia standard silver). Often these can be identified. Other occasional marks include the thistle on some Scottish sterling silver from 1750 and the Irish crowned harp.

Many articles made by silversmiths were exempted from marking from 1739, including filigree work, very rich ornament and much that weighed less than 10 pennyweights (less than five pennyweights from 1790).

Mazer-type bowl 1500 to 1520, and coconut cup, 1580. Such treasures can still be seen in a museum or college hall.

Early domestic silver. Silver marks are no more than a necessary preliminary to the fascinating study of silver plate. This must usually begin among the treasures (frequently gilded) that are found in museum or college hall. Domestic silver offers a wonderful commentary on social history because it was intended primarily for use, but this has meant scant respect for outmoded design.

The wonder is that so much silverware still remains from Tudor and early Stuart days, ranging from spoons with straight stems, knop-ended (acorn, seal, heraldic lion, widely reproduced maidenhead and apostle figure), to the standing salt and loving cup ceremonial symbols in early feasting, and the silver-mounted drinking horns, mazer bowls and coconut cups.

The well-to-do Stuart schoolboy took his own silver beaker and spoon and knife and the fork that gradually crept into 17th century fashion. Early drinking vessels were "raised." The silversmith rounded his vessel from the flat silver entirely by prolonged hammering with frequent heating to keep the metal workable. Ornament including

---

Below: bell salt, 1594, standing salt, 1563. Right: mid 17th c. tankards; two-handled embossed cup and cover, 1683.

engraved lines, embossing hammered from behind (repoussé) and work with small punches (chasing). In the shallow saucer vessel used by the wine taster, the embossed pattern aided scrutiny of the wine; the tankard had a solid ornamental casting as the thumb piece.

Post-Restoration glitter. Silver in pleasantly restrained design met many needs in wealthy 17th century households, including especially attractive covered cups, the pair of handles cast perhaps as caryatids, the lid shaped so that it could be inverted as a shallow dish on a stemmed foot. But a new era of silversmithing started when Charles II and his court returned from Holland in 1660 with new ideas of domestic comfort.

Among the more extravagant glitter, such as elaborate toilet sets, the collector notes sturdy pillar candlesticks on square bases, early vessels for coffee, tea and chocolate and a change to spoons with arching stems and notched, forward-curving ends.

The phrase William and Mary silver usually implies the important 1690s to 1700s happily associated with much

charming domestic silver, from the upright snuffer stand to the notch-rimmed monteith which contained iced water for cooling wine glasses.

Much silver was decorated merely with borders of the repetitive, light-catching knuckles known as gadrooning, with embossed and chased acanthus leaf borders and cast finials such as flames and melons and crouching lions. Plain-bodied casters were never more delightfully pierced than at this period.

But more adventurous design and ornament came with the arrival of the Huguenot refugee silversmiths, suggesting new ways of coping with the softer, purer silver that the smith had to use between 1697 and 1720.

Below: monteith of 1698, with characteristic undulating rim.
Right: shapely hot milk pot, 1702, and teapot on stand, 1710.

The real Queen Anne silver. Looking back, it is easy to see how the flamboyant late 17th century's somewhat heavy baroque silver design was transformed into the gracious style of Queen Anne silver. Anne reigned only from 1702 to 1714, but is associated with design through the first 20 years of the 18th century, and this matter of dating is further confused by the tendency to give her name to much silver of the Victorian period.

But there is a simple shapeliness about the real Queen Anne silver, in well balanced baluster outlines with high domed lids and curving swan-neck spouts. Even in minor items such as candlestick and caster, the baluster or pear shape prevailed; even plain surfaces at this period were beautifully

enriched with English silversmiths' renowned engraving.

The tea-making ritual was served by a particularly charming tea equipage. Water in a silver kettle was kept boiling on its stand over a lamp. The hostess unlocked the silver canister and made tea for each of her guests in a tiny teapot with a lidded spout. Cold milk was a late-comer to the tea table, but a covered silver sugar bowl was provided and slender tongs as well as silver spoons in their spoon dish. Perfect finishing touch to the equipage was a mote skimmer, its pierced spoon bowl skimming dust from the poured tea and its barbed end clearing tea leaves from inside the teapot spout.

As already mentioned, special hallmarks tell us when

Tea kettle on spirit lamp stand, 1715, and chocolate pot, 1703, strengthened by cut-card work in foliate pattern.

we encounter the soft, cool-toned Britannia standard silver compulsory for silversmiths at that time. Working it required especial skill. Ewers, tankards, covered cups, even casters and coffee pots, might be encircled with strengthening bands, often twinkling with gadroons. But a more imaginative development was the vertical corrugation of melon fluting that shapes the rounded body of many a kettle and teapot.

Possible weakness where spout or handle was attached to a vessel's curving body was met by cutcard work. A thin piece of silver cut in formal or foliate pattern was attached to the thin surface around the joint.

The bold elegance of early Georgian days. When silversmiths could use sterling silver once more, they worked it boldly. Strong, square outlines and substantial mouldings characterise typical pieces of the 1720s to 1730s like the rectangular tea canister with high-stepped lid, the popular small tray known as a waiter, the trencher salt with incurving sides and clipped concave corners.

This clipped corner outline was an alternative to the

Below: hexagonal candlestick, 1720; Scottish skittleball teapot, 1725. Right: extravagant rococo cream jug, 1750.

octagonal shaping that then gave character to the baluster outlines in every kind of silverware from the tea-table taperstick to the handle of the bell gracing the crisply-rimmed inkstand tray. Equally forthright was the sphere, for "bullet" tea kettle, sugar bowl and straight-sided teapot.

Rococo and chinoiserie. Inevitably, then, silversmiths found contrast of design in the wild extravaganza, French-inspired, that the 19th century dubbed rococo. Because silversmithing is primarily concerned with making shapely practical wares for those with an eye – and a purse – for sophisticated elegance, this rococo mood was particularly attractive, gay without absurdity.

Pleasure in ornament exquisitely chased was expressed in a wealth of scrolls and flowers and curving shells, in flowing, asymmetrical patterns. Sometimes the design contained cherubs or sea horses or romantic Gothic pillars, sometimes swirling flames and often Chinamen, pagodas and all the European notions of Chinese ornament now termed chinoiserie, minutely detailed on jaunty little salt cellars and sets of tea canisters. In tea ware this happy riot of ornament

appeared on teapots and kettles in inverted pear outline with fantastic spouts and on supremely collectable cream jugs, which were three-footed, with tip-tilted handle and spout. Small trays in this style often had their rims extravagantly cast and chased.

In early Georgian days even the tankard acquired a swelling tulip shape on a moulded foot-ring, with a double dome lid and a double scroll handle. Paul de Lamerie, at work in London 1711 to 1751, was so skilled in working the fine Britannia standard silver that he continued with it into the 1730s. Like Pierre Harache and Augustine Courtauld, he was of Huguenot descent.

Adam neo-classic grace. It must be stressed that much early Georgian silver was comparatively plain to meet domestic needs, but such work only emphasises the eager romantic mood of the day with forceful baluster outlines, boldly curving spouts and handles, ornate little feet on jug and salt cellar and gravy boat. Reaction from all this extravaganza was the more emphatic.

Soon after the mid 18th century came a new approval of

Below: Paul de Lamerie candelabrum, 1737. Right: ram's head ornament on 1774 candlestick; urn-like hot-water jug, 1775.

antiquity. More and more young men of fashion were touring Europe and could glimpse for themselves the wonders of classical civilisation and it was easy for such influential leaders of fashion as Robert Adam to win approval for his neo-classic ideals.

These, it must be stressed, were far from the solemn pomp of earlier and later classical revivals. Adam, who included silver among his designs for interior furnishings, wrote of novelty, variety and amusement. With his sphinxes and rams' heads, his bows and flower swags, he shared his pleasure in a light-hearted, romantic adaptation of classic design and ornaments that in lesser hands tended to become somewhat stereotyped.

In shape, all was curving grace. Tall, slender-footed pots for tea and coffee were given graceful urn outlines with high-shouldered handles and tapering spouts. Lidded jugs might be in amphora outline on tripod bases, favoured, too, for ornate candelabra. Candlesticks were square-based classic columns.

Workaday silver reflected such glories in graceful,

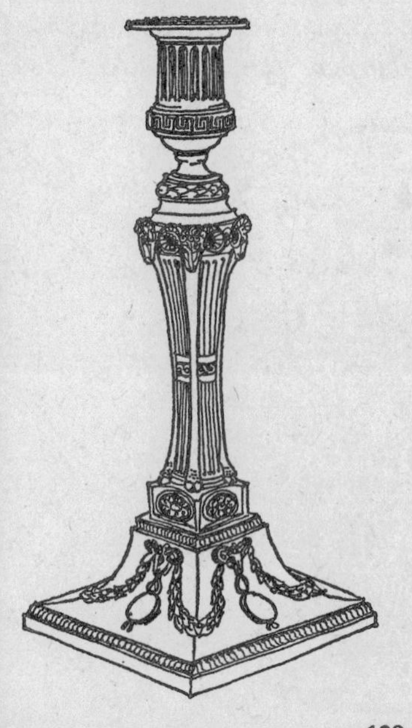

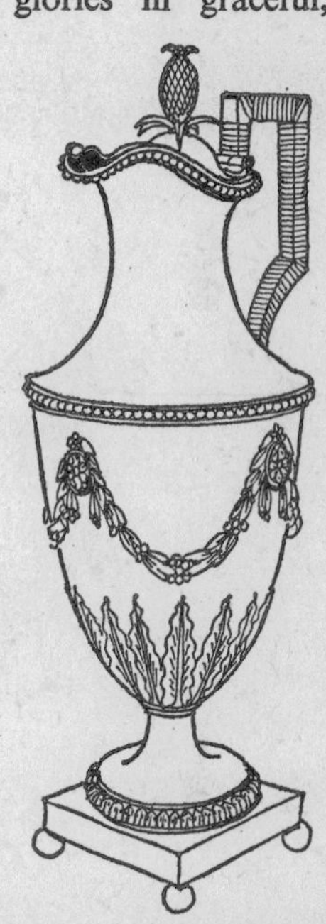

simple outlines and a range of "safe" neo-classic ornaments, immediately comparable with the Wedgwood ceramics then widely fashionable. Silversmiths had to meet demands by increasing numbers of customers who were new to such pleasures of gracious living and welcomed cheaper silver-substitutes.

To compete, many evolved factory methods of shaping and assembling their silver: hence modifications of neo-classic design to accept, for example, straight-sided teapots and caddies, often oval on plan. One has only to compare perforated work such as the 18th century's lovely baskets to see the saving in labour when regular machine-stamping took over from delicate hand sawing.

Characteristic details of the 1780s to 1790s include the shallow fluting that strengthened thin price-trimmed silver-ware. In contrast, a considerable weight of silver was clearly indicated by another fashionable form of ornament known as bright-cutting. At a period when table glass was beginning to sparkle with deep diamond-cutting, silversmiths used specially shaped gouges in order to cut away tiny facets

Below: glass-lined pierced sugar pail, 1772. Right: Sheffield plate sugar bowl; Hester Bateman salt and caster, 1780.

of metal and burnish the resultant hollows to a fine shine.

The famous Hester Bateman (widowed 1760, d. 1794) is associated with some of this work, but is perhaps over-estimated. Her workshops produced pleasant, medium quality work, including spoons which by then had gracefully arching stems and smoothly rounded ends, some in the waisted fiddle outline.

The challenge of Sheffield plate. Matthew Boulton, 1728 to 1809, was a progressive silversmith remembered also for silver's greatest rival, Sheffield plate. This English invention (in Sheffield, 1742) meant that silver wares could be imitated more cheaply in silver fused upon copper. Sheffield plate, rolled as thin as silver plate, was similarly raised, soldered, pierced, chased, die-stamped, drawn to make wire, and so on. (This is considered fully in the next chapter.)

When the copper was silvered on both sides, it still showed red copper edges masked with silver wire or, later, with cast or die-stamped mounts. Fron 1836, marks resembling silver hallmarks might be used on Sheffield plate, or on British plate with its whitish nickel alloy core.

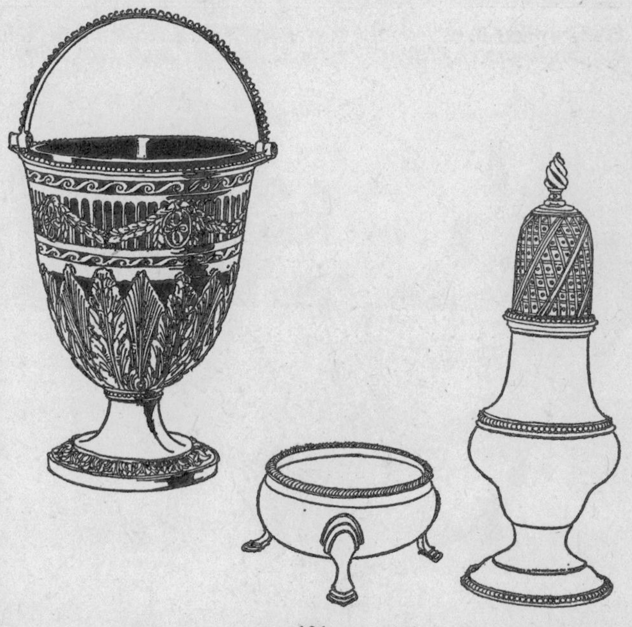

Regency Splendour. One answer to such unwelcome competition came from master silversmiths making immensely rich, magnificent silver, including vases, urns, candelabra, wine coolers and tureens, in the massive classical style associated with the Regency.

This new enthusiasm was fostered by much serious work on discoveries at Herculaneum, Pompeii and in Egypt. Silversmiths' designers and patrons revelled in imperial Roman grandeur and Egyptian symbolism. Especially important was Paul Storr, at work 1792 to 1821, whose craftsmanship is seen in ceremonial vessels with sculptural figures and animal supports on massive pedestals loaded with weightly castings, every detail perfectly worked.

Today, however, the collector of Regency silver may be attracted by an entirely different range of articles. Teapots with attendant milk and sugar vessels were never more pleasing, often almost plain in low, squat shape with a short spout and an upswept cape around the lid opening.

Among really tiny treasures, the collector looks for vinaigrettes, the decoratively lidded boxes filled with

Below: Regency teapots by Will Bateman, Jonathan Alleine; Paul Storr tureen. Right: "revived rococo" snuff box, 1846.

sponges soaked in aromatic vinegar, small enough for the daintiest reticule, the early ones with exquisitely pierced inner lids. Or there are tea caddy spoons and ladles shaped as tea leaves, shells and scoops. Some collectors search out pocket graters, still perhaps carrying fragments of nutmeg for spicing a glass of wine.

By the 1830s and 1840s, silver was expected to declare its value in florid embossing and casting, especially of flower and leaf, shell and scroll, that somehow lacked the vivacity of the previous century's rococo. Fat little bacchantes in high relief scrambled among fruiting vines on coasters for cut glass decanters and on tickets naming the liquors that hung round the decanters' necks.

But, again, the collector finds particularly interesting personal silver, in snuff boxes for table and pocket and in cases for visiting cards, often pleasingly textured with the formal line patterning known as engine-turning.

Those imaginative Victorians. Early Victorians combated the growing ugliness of their surroundings with wildly romantic home furnishings. Form may often appear to us

deplorable, overweighty towards the base like a crinolined lady, with grotesque oversize feet. But ornament is rich in imaginative, story-telling detail.

Most ambitious was presentation silver, plateaux for the table and caskets and inkstands for the library desk. Elaborate silver sculptures with people, animals and buildings rising from naturalistic vegetation were displayed at the 1851 Great Exhibition and were also considered appropriate reward both for civic dignitary and champion racehorse.

Impossible to polish, these items doubtless prompted the approval of contrasting frosted and burnished surfaces. Among useful silver, sometimes every part of a teapot's surface was embossed and chased with picture detail (Teniers was a long-favoured source and Moorish scenes had a brief vogue).

Lid, finial, spout and feet were figure castings. Ornament of flowers, insects and birds in high relief started the mid-century vogue for tea sets (for tea and coffee, cream and sugar), condiment sets, spoons, inkstands and chamber

---

Below: Dixon pitcher plant tea and coffee set, 1851. Right: Albert Wilms centrepiece; Felix Summerly christening cup.

candlesticks shaped as flowers, shells and so on. Long-popular melon shaping is most attractive.

By the 1850s, even such enduring naturalism as the vine-wreathed claret jug was a trifle outmoded but proved as enduring as Victorian "Elizabethan" borders or interlaced strapwork and oval cartouches.

Victorian silver testifies to the fact that its makers were marvellous craftsmen who worked to the orders of designers lacking practical knowledge of techniques. Behind them stood the customer, and critics had no hesitation in calling his taste deplorable. Attempts to improve it were led by the Society of Arts including especially Henry Cole whose Felix Summerly Art Manufactures from 1846 tried to associate "the best art with familiar objects in everyday use." One result was the decade's delight in appropriate ornament laboriously indicating its purpose at a time when exact replicas in silver – electrotypes – could be made mechanically.

Rival "electro-plate". If this association of artist and crafts man was important to the silversmiths, it became infinitely more urgent when a new range of customers discovered the

glittering splendour of silverware in far cheaper electroplated silver.

These confusing terms must be understood clearly. Articles made of sterling and Britannia silver are spoken of as silver plate. But Sheffield plate has its sterling silver surfaces fused to a core of copper. Plated silver, as patented by the Elkington company in 1840, is ware wholly constructed in a cheaper nickel alloy and finally masked by a thin coating of pure silver by an electrical process. A rubbed area may reveal the yellowish nickel, but the thrifty housewife determined to make a fine show could have her ware re-silvered (a process that ruins the value of old Sheffield plate). Plated silver is described in the next chapter.

For innumerable middling families it meant that delicately flavoured fish and fruits could be enjoyed long before stainless steel tablewares became available. For the collector it means that high quality Victorian design is encountered in far greater quantity. Electro-types spread exact knowledge of classical forms and decoration. Through the 1860s and 1870s fashionable coffee pots and claret jugs were long-

---

Below: Sheffield plate tray. Right: Greek influence in coffee pot and jug; William Burges medieval decanter, 1865.

necked versions of Greek vases. Contrast might be introduced by parcel (part) gilding. And instead of frosting, oxidising might give silver a complete range of tints from white to black.

In contrast to the continuing abundance of naturalistic ornament were contemporary harsh angular forms with occasional interesting exceptions, such as the original "medieval" designs of William Burges, 1827 to 1881. Much traditional work consisted of assemblies of over-lavish castings condemned by leaders like Owen Jones who urged flat, stylised pattern. The depression of the late 1870s hastened a return to lighter design, confusedly incorporating Adam and Regency features. Frames holding bottles, cruets, egg-cups-and-spoons are pleasant workaday pieces.

Among important reforming designers of "art silver" in the late 19th century was Christopher Dresser, 1834 to 1904, an enthusiast for newly discovered Japanese craftsmanship. His plain, functional work, using a minimum of material, sometimes suggests the starkness of machinery. Others include the more persuasive C.R. Ashbee, Philip Webb, C.F.A.

Voysey and Gilbert Marks. As a commercial venture, somewhat clumsy-looking Cymric silver was sold from 1899, hand-hammered, gleaming with a soft sheen and decorated with Celtic detail or semi-precious stones.

For the general public, silverwork was still machine dominated – cast and stamped and spun into confusions of 18th century styles unhelpfully called "Queen Anne."

Turn of the century. Factory requirements continued to dominate production methods. Tea, milk and sugar vessels for example, show modified Regency forms, oval or oblong on plan, the thin silver strengthened on the lower part of the body with vertical reeding.

Sales catalogues of the period offer a fascinating range of minor wares from egg steamer to grape scissors. Some tall Art Nouveau shapes proved acceptable, tapering upwards from flat base to flat lid and with stylised, writhing plant ornament. But most commercial silver followed Victorian notions of 18th century designs such as "rococo" salt cellars. Tea caddies and the like embossed with all-over flower patterning were "old English."

Plain egg-shaped electro-plate tea set, 1880, typifies the reforming influence of some late 19th century "art silver".

6. SHEFFIELD PLATE

Copper coins minted in Roman London might glimmer with a silver coating. So great is silver's appeal that through subsequent centuries men tried many ways of applying the precious metal over iron, steel, copper and various base metal alloys.

This might aim to suggest the beautiful craftwork of the silversmith but, at a practical level, harness might thus be protected from rust, or urn taps be protected from corrosion, and the fastidious diner's cutlery was, by this coating, made safe from tainting the subtle flavours of such foods as fruit or fish.

The ancient idea of wrapping the base metal in layer upon layer of thinly beaten silver leaf eventually became practical

Epergne, with elaborately pierced dishes for sweetmeats, of the late 18th c., Sheffield plate's most important period.

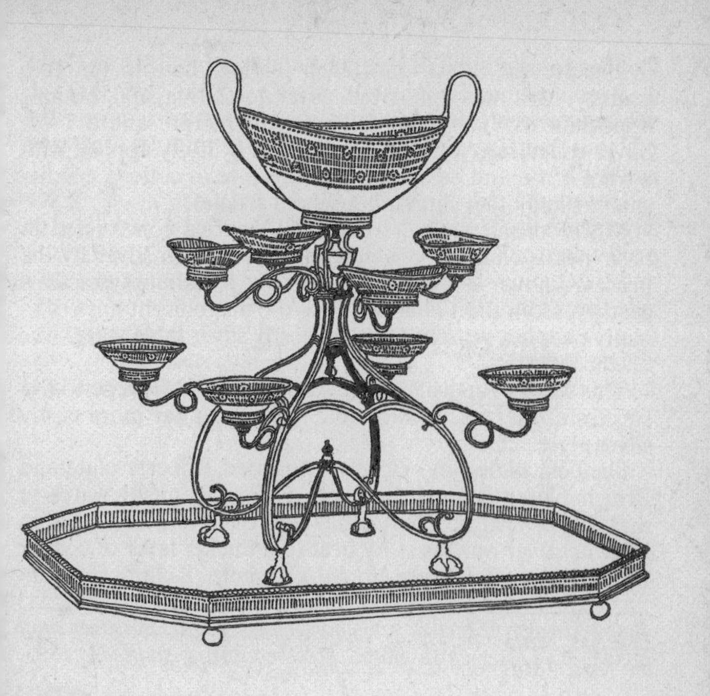

in the process known as french plating. Late in the 18th century, this was improved as close-plating and became important in Sheffield and Birmingham from about 1805. Silver rolled into a filmy-thin foil was skilfully applied with a trace of tin and great heat and pressure to cutlery, candle-snuffers and other similar household articles.

More conspicuously, from 1840, articles constructed in base metals could be covered completely with silver by the process known as electro-plating. But for almost exactly a century, from the 1740s to 1840s, the magnificent answer to many people's yearning for less costly silver table wares was Sheffield plate.

This wholly English notion was unique and for a period so successful that Sheffield set the fashion for far more costly silver plate.

Sheffield plate (and closely associated Roberts plate and British plate) differed from other silvered metal wares in that the silvering process came before manufacture. A thin layer of silver was fused by heat to a thicker layer of copper while both metals were brick-like ingots. Rolling into flat

Below: Joseph Hancock saucepan, 1750s. Right: Bolsover snuff boxes, c. 1750; close-plated steel eccentric snuffers, 1807.

sheets left the copper evenly covered with a thinner layer of sterling silver.

For the first time, the great status symbol of silver brilliance in ornament and tableware could be paraded in innumerable middle class homes in work that for years would be virtually indistinguishable from the much more expensive silver plate.

The new techniques. It is the delight of collectors today to discover the small differences and so to identify Sheffield plate. But at the time only the makers knew just how different and how much more difficult it was at every stage of manufacture to raise and seam, to pierce and chase and engrave this cheaper fused plate.

The process originated with Thomas Bolsover, 1704 to 1788 – his spelling of his name, though some spell it Boulsover – of Sheffield. He began in 1742 by making buttons and advanced no further than such small wares as snuffboxes and buckles.

It was left to his apprentice Joseph Hancock to extend the range of techniques and sophistication of products.

Advantages and problems. Like moulded glass and pinchbeck jewellery and the 18th century's other gay pretences, Sheffield plate was enormously successful because it was comparatively cheap. In 1784, when the silversmith's costs were increased by a tax of sixpence an ounce (one shilling and sixpence by 1815), pieces made of Sheffield plate could be sold at one third of his prices.

But what problems it entailed. At first the silver covered the copper on only one side. Hollow ware was tinned inside and some articles were made from two sheets of Sheffield plate placed back to back.

From about 1765, it was usual to fuse an ingot of silver to each face of the copper, but even then, every article, from

---

Below: elegant sauce tureens of the 1770s. Right: an Adam-style hot-water jug and gadrooned coffee pot made in 1780s.

ornate epergne to simple tankard, still required a mask of silver to be applied on every cut edge where the copper showed as a raw red line.

Using the silversmith's techniques, the manufacturer raised his bowls and saucers by long hammering and annealing and shaped their edges inch by inch in a steel-jawed swage. But he always had to watch lest he damage the delicate silver surface. Final burnishing had to leave the ware impeccably smooth and bright.

But those raw copper edges long proved a special difficulty to overcome. They soon revealed the underlying colour when early Sheffield plate men merely turned them over or masked them with silver solder.

Early wares. The solution to this problem really decided the success of Sheffield plate. At first the platers thought they had found it when George Whateley patented Sheffield plate wire, an astonishing small achievement.

Just as silver wire could be drawn out gradually from an inch-thick rod, so fused copper and silver produced copper wire entirely encased in silver, and this could be flattened to form a ribbon without revealing its red core.

When, by the 1780s, this, too, proved vulnerable as an edging, the platers used costlier solid silver wire. But by then Sheffield plate was securely established as part of the English neo-classic scene.

Candlesticks, for instance, were never more splendid

Candlesticks, 1780, one a "Corinthian" column, the other shouldered with an urn candlesocket. Behind, a dish cross.

than in the 1770s when Sheffield designers out-classed tradition-bound silversmiths. Many a handsome specimen remains today, its Corinthian pillar rising from a square plinth. By the 1780s, a shouldered, tapering pillar might be topped by an urn candlesocket, with ornament on all parts in deep relief. The Sheffield plate candelabrum was especially impressive, with its central socket supporting two or more socket-ended arms scrolling or twisting around a central finial.

For smokers and letter sealing, the Sheffield plate wax-jack offered an open stand supporting a spool and waxpan for a coil of flexible wax taper, giving a glimmer of light that burnt out safely if forgotten. Another interesting item

Below: gravy argyles with low set spouts and (inside) hot-water compartments. Right: horizontal, vertical wax-jacks.

introduced as early as the 1770s was the gravy argyle, suggesting a teapot with a low set, excessively slender spout. Inside, either a hot-water compartment or a box iron (which had been heated beforehand in the kitchen fire) ensured that guests could serve themselves to the best of the gravy while it was still piping hot.

The box iron was long favoured for heating magnificent Sheffield plate urns; but for hot serving dishes another early Sheffield plate suggestion was the dish cross.

This had four horizontal, pivoting arms which radiated from a central spirit lamp. Each arm was fitted with a bracket that was linked to a small foot, and these could be moved along the arms to hold any size of dish rim.

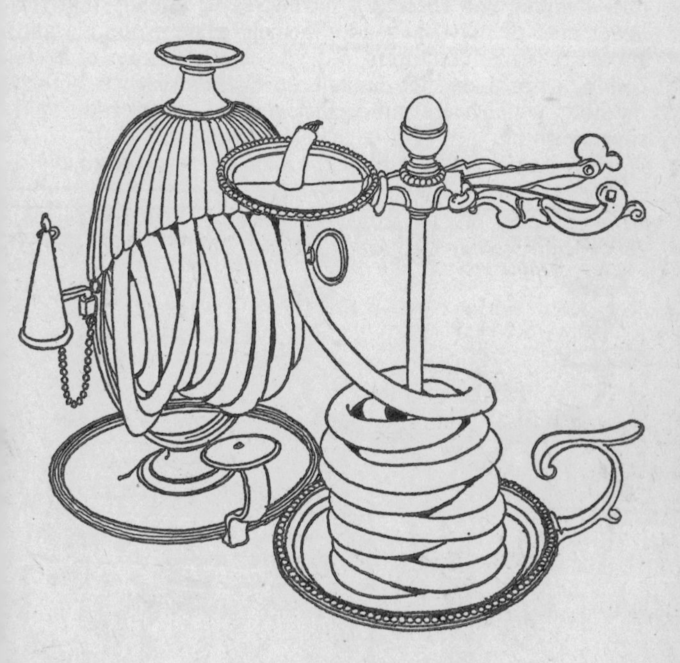

Marks. Early Sheffield plate seldom offers the collector any helpful marks. As early as 1773, silversmiths felt sufficiently threatened to have a law passed that banned marks of any kind on their upstart rival; and when marks were permitted, from 1784, they had to include the maker's name in full. Since these could never resemble silver hallmarks, few makers registered or used them.

When marks are found on Sheffield plate, they are most likely to indicate Victorian work. Superficially similar British plate, from 1836, was often marked with unregistered devices much like silver hallmarks. Occasionally, too, a collector finds a crown mark to distinguish Sheffield plate from poor quality continental work that was imported after 1815.

Die-stamping and chasing. I have stressed already that the lower cost of material made Sheffield plate profitable and encouraged manufacturers to devise elaborate ways of overcoming its problems. Ornament especially prompted factory methods which were more efficient than much traditional silversmithing.

Always with Sheffield plate the main concern was to avoid

Below: double-slide telescopic candelabrum, Richard Morton, 1800; flat-chased tea caddy. Right: 1812 table centre.

breaking or bruising or cutting through the thin silver surface and revealing the copper. This ruled out at once all normal engraving.

Instead, some of the patterns were flat-chased with small punches expertly tapped.

But even for much of such low-relief work, and for all deep relief or repoussé ornament, the Sheffield plate men soon found it most effective to press the fused metal with stamping hammers into dies cut in blocks of cast steel. The steel was hardened after it had been hollowed into a number of delicately detailed patterns.

By this method, for example, the stem of a pillar candlestick could be decorated all over in relief before being curled into a tube and vertically seamed.

Obviously, silversmiths made it as hard as possible for Sheffield plate to imitate their fashionable patterns. By the 1780s, when extraordinarily clear cut Sheffield plate ornament was die-stamped in high relief, the silversmiths turned to the scintillating, sharp-angled engraving known as bright-cutting. But even bright-cutting could be closely simulated

in Sheffield plate by expert die-stamping and chasing.

Some engraving, such as family crests, was inescapable. In early work, a salver might have a hole cut and filled with a piece of silver where the engraving would come. Soon the silver was merely soldered over the surface, and eventually it was found that a circle or rectangle of pure silver could be "rubbed in" until it seemed to become part of the surface. (This area may be detected when tarnished, for only pure silver could adhere and the silver of Sheffield plate is of sterling quality.)

Sometimes you can see a pinprick marking the centre of such an area as a guide to the engraver. He would probably be a specialist who was employed by the shop which sold the ware.

Ambitious ornament. Perforated pattern was another problem, which may be why silversmiths delighted in pierced cake baskets, dish rings, decanter coasters and vessels such as sugar and cream pails with the piercing set off by linings of blue glass.

Nevertheless, despite the prospect of all those tiny red

Below: splendidly pierced, swing-handled cake basket. Right: fish slice, 1790s, and perforated "potato ring", about 1785.

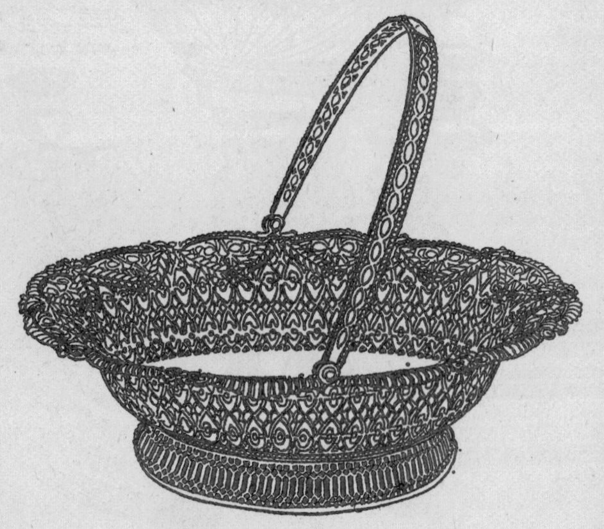

edges, Sheffield plate men produced all these charming items, too, and many more. They could not use the silversmith's hand fretsaw, but another tool was devised – a fly-punch consisting of a piercing tool and a steel bed that exactly fitted it.

Hole by hole, the sheet of Sheffield plate was pierced before the piece was assembled, the tool being used to drag down the silver over the sides of the perforation.

The mid 1780s to early 1790s was a wonderful period for superb Sheffield plate, marred only by the effect of war upon the export market. From about 1785, when solid silver satisfactorily masked the edges, makers could indulge in ambitious ornamental designs.

Among the most splendidly elaborate was the epergne, or table centre, which originated in silver, for offering sauces and spices. An open frame on four scrolling legs supported a central dish, while around it rose scrolling branches carrying small dishes similarly chased and pierced. These might hold fruits or sweetmeats; sometimes, if required, they could be exchanged for candle sockets.

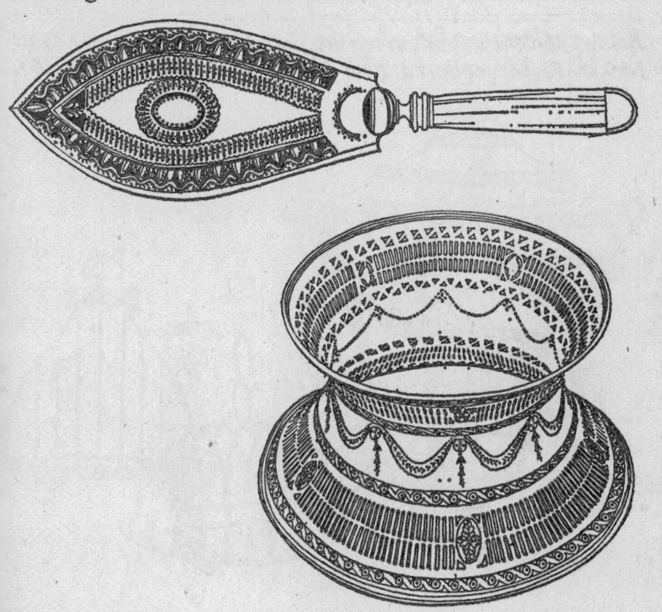

Wire work. In an early epergne even the handles of the small basket dishes would be punch-perforated hole by hole. But an obvious alternative was to construct the basket – or toast rack, cruet stand or many another lightweight article – entirely in Sheffield plate wire, and set it off magnificently by a lining of blue glass.

This wire, which could be rolled into flat ribbon, was an ideal material for fashioning small basket handles and sugar tongs and other little details where soldered-on edges would be clumsy. Wire making was improved about 1780 and perfected about 1800.

At first a vessel might be composed of short, U-shaped wires fixed between rim and base by drilled holes and solder; early in the 19th century came S-shaped wires, followed by a continuous wire pattern – and followed, too, by several less perfectly soldered modern imitations.

Sheffield plate, like silver in the years around the end of the century, showed many contrasts between this lightweight work and such substantial pieces as tea and coffee sets with hot water, cream and sugar vessels arranged on ornate tea

Below: Matthew Boulton tea urn, late 18th c.; wire-work toast racks. Right: collared oval shapes for an 1810 tea set.

trays. The late 18th century's severe, straight-sided teapots gave place to the extremely attractive, low-bodied oval teapot with a flaring collar around the lid opening, a most lively and attractive shape which all too soon expanded into a drooping outline.

For the connoisseur's coffee, the period's vessel was the squat, straight-sided, lamp-supported coffee biggin, fitted inside with a fabric filter like a small child's biggin cap. But most handsome of all were the urns (and remember that guests would see the imposing "classic" outline and the clumsy tap was hidden at the back). The wide bowl shape was never bettered and suited the heavy reeding or gadrooning on lid, body and ball-footed plinth characteristic of the period.

From about 1790, lavish ornament on such a piece might include decorative silver mounts such as scrolls and shells. Sheffield plate could not be cast, of course, so it came most naturally to these manufacturers to die-shape such mounts far more cheaply from thin silver and then weight them with molten solder.

Late Georgian contrasts. Many a guest, seeing such gleaming ornament on tea tray or wine cooler, must have been persuaded that the ware was costly silver through and through.

Sheffield plate men were so alert to this enjoyment of harmless deception that they might fit an ornate egg-cup stand with a set of egg cups (that the breakfast guest would be able to scrutinise closely) made of hall-marked silver.

But this pompous, wealth-flaunting attitude to weighty silver encouraged by master silversmiths was of little real service to the Sheffield plate manufacturer, despite many an ornate inkstand loaded with silver mounts. His table candlesticks for instance, lost their fine neo-classic grace in favour of

Below: 1805 cheese toaster in Sheffield Museum. Right: a Sheffield plate frame might hold silver egg cups and spoons.

massive ornament on socket, shoulder and heavily weighted base. An ingenious design is the straight, squat-looking stick, not always recognised as a telescopic piece able to double its height.

One trouble for Sheffield plate manufacturers was the high cost of the elaborate dies that shaped the fused metal. It became tempting to continue outmoded patterns. A way to cut costs was to follow another method long practised by factory silversmiths and shape hollow ware by spinning.

By the 1820s, copper was available that was pliant enough for a sheet of Sheffield plate to be revolved on a lathe against a wooden form that gradually forced it into the required shape.

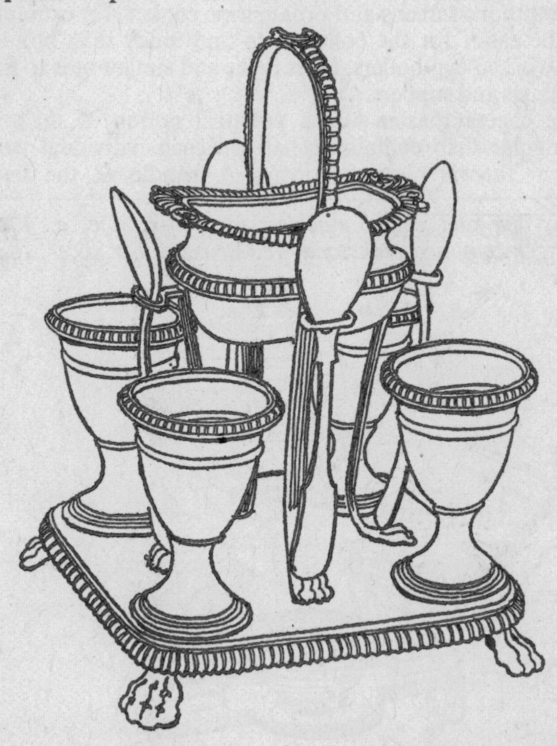

Practical service. Spun work, thin and vulnerable, is despised by some collectors. But at least this period's price-cutting thin plate prompted appealing, dent-withstanding designs such as melon-shaping, fluting and reeding. The great range of styles and qualities in regency and late Georgian plate can only be realised when you take the trouble to examine a collection such as the display in the Sheffield City Museum.

Designers must have been as confused as we may be by the renewed interest in contrasting Greek and rococo shapes and increasing demand for laboriously naturalistic detail. But such a collection indicates, too, how much plain Sheffield plate was made for everyday service.

Sumptuous tureens and ornate wine coolers, for example, may be easier for the collector to find today than homely hard-worked egg-boilers, toast racks and similar aids to fine breakfasts and suppers.

The cheese toaster was a practical notion, a shallow, rectangular dish containing half a dozen individual pans over a hot-water compartment. A handle at the back

---

Below: tea and coffee machine for self-service, c. 1800. Right: "locomotive" inkstand, 1830s; cucumber slicer, 1820.

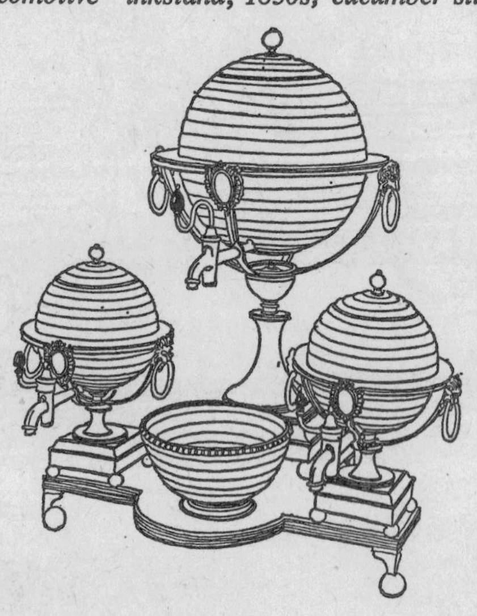

enabled it to be thrust towards the fire, the cook's hand protected by a hinged lid held half-open by a chain. The lid perfectly reflected the fire's heat on to rounds of toast piled with cheese that could be browned while lying flat in their small pans.

A tube and blade device for slicing fresh cucumber at table is another intriguing Sheffield Museum exhibit, and self service again was offered by the Sheffield plate tea-and-coffee machine. This consisted of an urn mounted over a spirit lamp that swivelled to replenish either of two smaller urns, all of them grouped on a stand with a basin for dregs.

One of these machines in Sheffield Museum has the name and churchwarden pipe mark used by Daniel Holy, Wilkinson & Co. Such a mark is an unexpected bonus, although a quality mark is sometimes noted, like the SILVER EDGES used by Matthew Boulton.

A few firms indicated the proportion of silver to copper in the fused plate. By the century's end this was about one to 15 and soon became lower still.

Arrival of nickel silver. By the 1840s, hard hit Sheffield plate makers might skimp their silver until it was down to a proportion of one to 50. But by then their once popular manufacture had nearly ceased.

The first challenge came from Roberts plate in 1830. A whitish alloy of copper, zinc and nickel, known as nickel silver, was introduced between the silver and the copper. Tough British plate followed in 1836, with nickel silver replacing the copper.

Familiar Sheffield plate items continued to be made by the old methods, but the new alloy is easily recognised where the rub of wear shows a cold, yellowish-grey metal instead of mellow copper.

The real change came in 1840, when several men's far-sighted experiments culminated in a patent taken out by the Elkington brothers for what we know as electro-plate. Articles were constructed in nickel silver and an electrical process covered them with minute particles of pure silver. This silver frosting had to be scratch-brushed and polished to a faultless surface. The process was improved,

Below: British plate ice pail; electro-typed, silver plated taper stick, 1844. Right: EPNS dessert service, 1868.

making the power-driven polishing less arduous, but the essential difference remained.

In Sheffield plate, sterling silver was fused by heat upon copper before manufacturing processes began. In electro-plate, pure silver was added last, so that it masked all constructional detail. The letters EPNS often mark such plate (electro-plated nickel silver).

Elkington table wares. Early Victorians adored presentation trophies and table ornaments fashioned as factual, three-dimensional scenes. By Elkington electrical processes the most elaborate figure could be copied exactly in every detail (called an electrotype) and then electro-plated in pure silver.

At the Great Exhibition in 1851 electro-plating was hailed for its ornamental possibilities rather than for the inexpensive table elegance we think of today. (For tarnish-free surfaces of gold it avoided the appalling health hazards involved in gilding by mercury.) But Elkington price lists, issued between 1855 and 1862, already showed a huge range of table wares. Styled "rich

Elizabethan", "Arabesque", and the like, this electro-plate ranged from a seven guinea claret jug to fiddle pattern teaspoons at 16 shillings a dozen. Table forks very strongly plated and with silver points were £3 5s. a dozen – more for more ornate patterns.

Teapots were offered in all the patterns of their day from low cushion shapes to the tall, straight-sided vessel with melon swellings or vaguely Gothic detail. For those of pretended wealth the firm boasted "All mustards and casters have silver tops, Hall marked." At the same time they suggested that the money saved by not buying silver plate would earn interest in seven years that would pay for similar goods in electro-plate.

From prestige to functional. The Elkingtons, who were leading silversmiths as well, employed continental designers in the exuberant manner of the 1840s. Even in electro-plate they could offer a prestige piece such as a 30 guinea epergne with stags on a rocky base around a tree hung with glass dishes, or with cherubs among vines, or a group of "Moorish" Arabs and date palms.

Below: Elkington and (right) James Dixon teapots, c. 1850. Right: tree candelabrum, Elkington, 1855 and Dresser teapot.

But through the 1870s and 1880s a number of reforming influences affected even commercial design. Shapes became taller and plainer long before end-of-the-century Art Nouveau, including stemmed, tall-handled vessels for tea and coffee engraved with classical figure scenes. Pleasant urn outlines might be exaggerated into more angular shapes, and some narrow-necked, wide-based vessels were given ugly V-shaped handles.

This was a period of many interesting and conflicting moods, far beyond the old contrasts of classic grace and rococo frivolity. Japanese design became important, including plant shapes, and the reforming zeal of dedicated men like Sir Henry Cole began to have effect. This was expressed with special clarity in the starkly functional designs for both silver and electro-plate by Christopher Dresser, 1834 to 1904. His designs may be seen in work by Elkingtons, by the Sheffield firm of James Dixon and Sons and by Hukin and Heath of Birmingham.

Middle class value. End-of-century catalogues show an enormous range of electro-plated table wares. Novelties

included the four-footed breakfast dish whose revolving domed lid slid out of the way under the dish, an idea that spread to butter pots, egg steamers and so on. There saw silver-mounted cut glass: claret jugs, biscuit barrels, salad bowls, celery vases and arrays of toilet bottles. And all this could be matched in electro-plate (though it is hard to imagine who bought all the knife rests shaped as greyhounds, sphinxes and the like).

Prices emphasise the value of such goods to the middle class family, being less than half or even a third those of silver. In the 1890s, electro-plating on Britannia metal was far cheaper even than on nickel silver. Always there was the advantage that worn goods could be re-plated, a tea and coffee set costing no more than £1 or so, including regilding inside cream and sugar vessels.

By then Sheffield plate was all but forgotten. Strangely, just as buttons were among the first items made by Bolsover's new process in 1743, so they were among the last, early this century. The last, that is, until collector interest brought inevitable modern reproductions.

Simple functional cream jug and coffee pot designed by W. A. S. Benson, 1905, in contrast to the period's novelties.

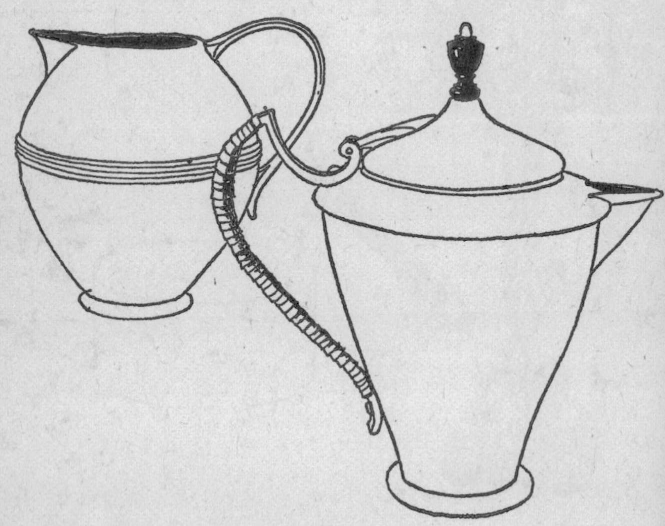

7. PEWTER & BRASS

For centuries brass and pewter gleamed a welcome into mansion, farmhouse and merchant's villa, precious as palace gold and silver plate. All who could afford the comfortable luxury turned to these clean, sturdy wares for the furnishing of table and kitchen, for lamp and candlestick and innumerable personal treasures from pipe stopper and snuff box to hand warmer and coat button.

Only during the past 200 years have ordinary folk been offered pleasant, serviceable, everyday earthenware, table glass and plated silver pieces.

But pewter and brass remain from Roman Britain; by the 14th century they were controlled by powerful guilds and, throughout those centuries that matter to today's

Below: 17th c. bronze posnet, 15th c. skillet. Right: bellied and bun top flagons; maidenhead, writhen ball knop spoons.

collectors – the 1600s to the 1900s, Britain was at the centre of Europe's metal working.

Pewter and brass are alloys. Just as silver was toughened with a trace of copper, so was silvery tin to make the finest quality pewter. Brass is a mixture of copper and zinc. Both met unwelcome competition with impressive improvements in quality and manufacturing methods that aid the collector with dating.

Inevitably, reproductions abound. Old pewter was "discovered" early this century and many early rarities were copied. Brass copies often go back no farther than mid Victorian horse brasses, yet even these are often betrayed by a careless finish no Victorian would have tolerated.

Pewter. Guild rules were strict for early pewterers, the sadware men who made plates, tankard and flagon makers long known as potters, spoonmakers and triflers responsible for minor articles such as buckles. The temptation was to make the alloy easier to work by adding lead: this ley metal eventually became so poisonous that a law in 1907 limited lead content to 10 per cent.

A garnish of early pewter is every collector's dream – a set of a dozen each of platters, large plates and bowls. Tin and temper – tin which was hardened with a little copper and bismuth or, later, antimony – made this gleaming flatware, which required no surface ornament save the occasional triangle of initials on a marriage plate. Variously

Below: pewter capstan salt, tankard, 1680s. Right: 17th c. candlesticks – salt-based, with corrugated stem, bell-based.

reeded rims date only from the late 17th century onwards.

Compulsory makers' marks made it possible for the guild to identify early pewter and records of a few of these "touches" remain. London especially retained quality control well into the 18th century, which explains the mark "London made." But it must be admitted that tiny punch marks beside the maker's mark were deceitfully intended to suggest silver hallmarks.

These may include EPBM on late Victorian wares (many of which were Georgian in style) originally electro-plated with silver. Factory and pattern registration numbers, too, were used during the 19th century and are not to be mistaken for dates of manufacture.

Brass and bronze. Early writers frequently confused yellow brass with the brownish alloy of copper, tin and zinc that is bronze. This included gun metal and bell metal, as important as brass to the powerful Founders' Guild, but supplied little about the house save an occasional posnet, cauldron or mortar.

Medieval brassmen were called potters when they cast their metal into cooking and serving vessels. Others, called latteners, noisily hammered brass ingots into sheets for flatware. Early latten in church memorial plates offers fascinating glimpses of life and costume from the 13th century. England had water-driven battery hammers flattening brass in the 1580s but much fine latten neverthe-

17th c. brass hanging chandelier was cast in parts: sockets, grease pans, scrolling arms and central globe and finial.

less continued to be imported until the early 18th century.

The collector can develop an eye for the colour and texture of early brass by examining museums' specimens. The hanging chandelier, for instance, was made for church and livery hall and cast in parts – sockets, grease pans, finely scrolling arms and a shapely central body topped by an ornamental finial and based in a hollow reflective globe. Countless kitchen vessels and tools included long-handled skimmers and three-footed saucepans (posnets) required for the open down-hearth. The curfew, shaped as a quarter sphere, recalls the medieval edict that such fires should be covered at night. Early brass lanterns may have cheap glass bull's eye panels.

Below: Earl of Essex brass warming pan. Right: snuffers and stand, 1700, baluster candlestick, 1680, wall sconce, 1706.

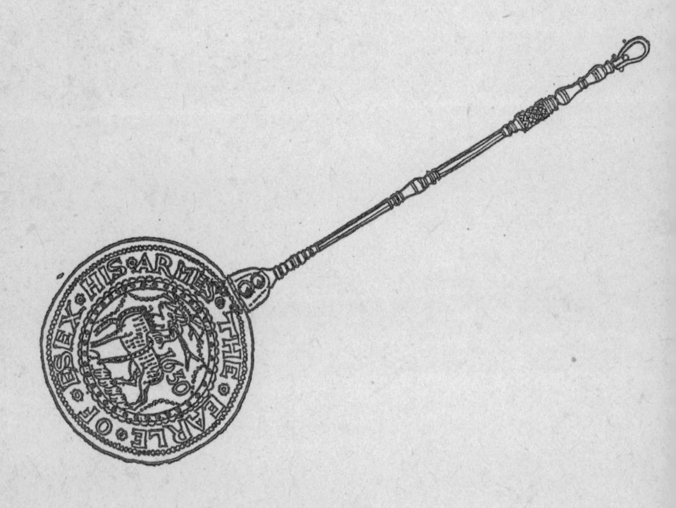

The importance of moulds. Pewter and brass contributed richly to the 17th and early 18th century home. Wall shelves would be bright with pewter; embossed brass magnified the light of candles in scrolling wall sconces and everywhere there would be candlesticks, with snuffers to trim the candles' wicks and douters to extinguish them.

The ways these pieces are made are important to the collector, who quickly sees that casting was at the heart of most early work. Molten metal was poured into moulds so costly that they often had to be hired from the guilds.

Even pewter plates were cast before being trimmed in the lathe and hand hammered to make the metal compact and rigid, especially around the curve of the bouge. A

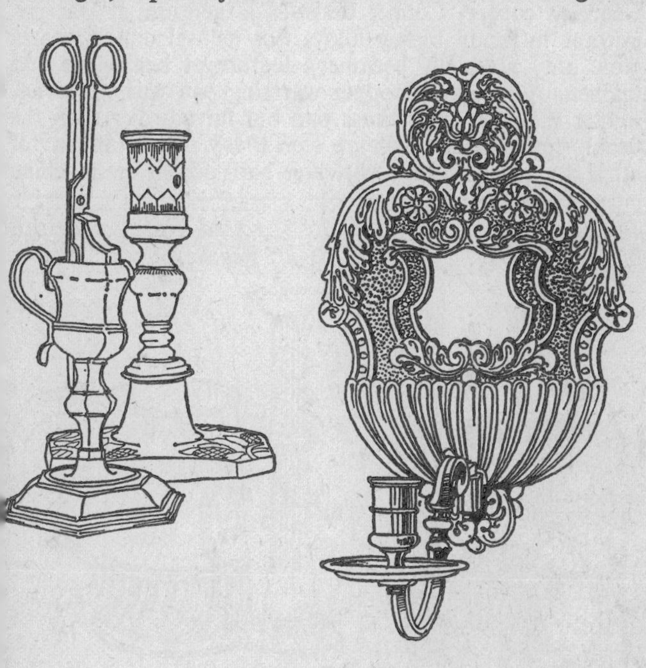

final smoothing and burnishing then obliterated marks from the upper surface.

Where necessary, a piece could be soldered (paling to the pewterer and brazing to the brassman). For instance, a 17th century candlestick would be cast in parts and finished by lathe-turning. In pewter, the base might serve also for casting salt cellers (see page 169).

Like silver, the earliest brass and pewter spoons had gay little cast finials – lion, acorn, maidenhead – soldered to straight stems and well hammered, fig-shaped bowls. In the 17th century, these were followed by notched, flattened ends, including treasured rarities cast with embossed surface ornament.

Georgian copper. Copper deserves a mention. It was important in many brassy alloys but its welcoming, warm glow only gradually became a feature of hearthside and kitchen. A Georgian copper warming pan was somewhat lighter than the early brass pan but far sturdier than the usual reproductions that are seen today. Most familiar of all is the one with the "beefeater hat" lid; in the machine

Below: brass lantern clock, 1665; raised brass candlestick and pewter mug, both 1680s. Right: Regency copper tea urn.

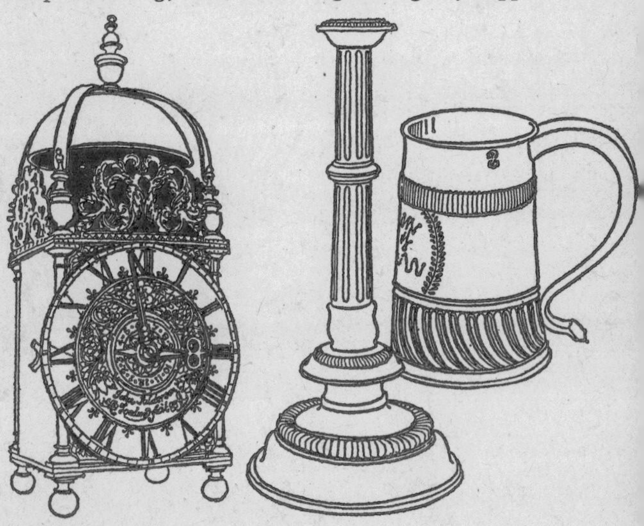

stamped copper the lid rim fits inside the ember pan rim.

Saucepans and fish kettles were made in copper, too, all of course needing frequent interior tinning. But more vessels, such as handsome tea urns, date mainly after 1820 when the supply of copper was no longer restricted by the requirements of war.

Ingenious ornament. Accepting copper's minor role, pewter and brass shared with iron all the duties of increasingly sophisticated domesticity through Stuart and early Georgian days. Design pleases us with its simplicity; nevertheless, there is much ingenious ornament for the collector to watch for, while avoiding later additions.

Early pewterers were fined occasionally for attempts to gild their wares. But colour on brass is found in very occasional enamelling; candlesticks and the like were cast with tiny surface hollows that were filled with enamel colours. More effective in brass and pewter was raised ornament, influenced by silversmiths who gave sparkle to candlestick or tankard with the repetitive swelling known as gadroons. Occasionally, some 17th century castings

show quite intricate ornament in relief on porringer or spoon. Repoussé tooling may be a later addition.

The engraver's ornament of delicate lines cut into the metal surface was largely restricted to brass, for instance on clock faces. In pewter such engraving soon became indistinct so may have been more common than we know. As early as Elizabethan days the Pewterers' Guild twice fined a man for employing a woman (who was not a guild member) to engrave his ware.

The work that has lasted is mainly the crude wriggled or joggled decoration with outlines chipped out in tiny zigzags. Derisive silver engravers called this practice "scratching". Even simpler repetitive patterns were made

Handsome 18th c. pewter punch bowl shows wriggled or joggled work. Pierced work on brass sugar dredger imitates silver.

sometimes on both pewter and brass with hammer and tiny punches, but far more interesting decoration was created by perforating the metal.

In pewter wares this is found in the cast handles of the small bowls usually called porringers and in the vertical thumbpiece or lever that gives character to the lidded tankard.

In brass, some of the most splendid work was done on locks and keys; chamberlains' keys-of-office, for instance, and superb lockplates where surface engraving might be combined with delicate cast tracery.

Closely following gilded silver, brass was perforated in the dainty arabesque patterns that were popular in the early 18th century. Such vessels include casters and the spherical wash-ball or soap holders found on early wash-basin stands.

Most familiar of all, perhaps, are the brass handles on Stuart and Georgian furniture, from the cast drops of Charles II's day to the bail handles and back plates and key escutcheons that became increasingly ornate towards

Below: William and Mary pewter porringer; finely pierced and decorated brass door lock. Right: pinchbeck châtelaine.

the 1760s and then retreated into neo-classic simplicity. A little superb brass inlay, too, is found on early Georgian mahogany furniture – foretaste of Regency inlay.

It may include the fine lines known as stringing, and in the early 18th century, stringing of pewter, too, was being practised by at least one firm, Coxed and Woster.

Prince's metal. The Victoria and Albert Museum has a splendid desk of about 1745 with lavish cast and gilded brass corner mounts; but gilding was only one early way that men sought to improve brass. In the 17th century, a type with more copper in proportion to the zinc was known as Prince Rupert's metal or prince's metal.

This was not very different from the invention of Christopher Pinchbeck, watchmaker, who probably used tutenag, the refined Chinese zinc that lined cases of tea. Pinchbeck was widely advertised by Christopher's son, 1733 to 1747.

It was slow to tarnish and popular for inexpensive jewellery and bijouterie. But soon the name was applied indiscriminately to articles made of cheaply gilded brass.

Pewter hollow ware. The early 18th century was a great period for fine pewter ware that still becomes available from time to time. The range is wide, including more plates, saucers (still for serving sauce) and the little dishes hired out for informal parties – dessert or banqueting dishes. Pewter, pleasantly smooth and clean to the lips, was specially valued for drinking vessels, the old guild rules stipulating that all interiors must be lathe burnished.

Vessels include the church flagon, important from the 1600s, tall, broad-skirted and tapering, with decorative thumbpiece and lid finial and, in the 18th century, sometimes an elaborate double-scroll handle.

Georgian tankards include the waisted tulip shape associated with West Country pewter, with a domed cover and curl or double curl to the tail of the handle that continued into early Victorian days. The open thumbpiece with cut-away centre was a favourite in the 18th century, before the tankard lost its final style of rimless lid.

A vessel that was restricted wholly to pewter was the

Below: 18th c. pewter standish. Right: 18th c. salt, domed tulip tankard; baluster, tappit hen, pot-bellied wine measures.

flat-lidded baluster wine measure, which can be dated roughly by the style of its thumbpiece and lid attachment. Careful scrutiny can suggest to the collector at least half a dozen ways in which its design helped the customer to detect any reduction in its size, such as dents made by a cunning barman.

The pot-bellied or pear-shaped measure was a Scottish variant with a lid like an inverted saucer; this is rarer today than the tappit hen. This popular name has been applied to measures of all capacities, but strictly meant a Scottish pint (three Imperial pints); the two smaller measures were the chopin and mutchkin.

The tappit hen has a much deeper vertical rim than the English measure, and instead of the smooth baluster swell the body has a concave curve down to a low waist and below this is vertical-sided again.

A standish was an early name for a writing box. Typically, this had compartments for quills and a penknife, vessels for ink and pounce (powder to check flow of ink), and sometimes also equipment for sealing letters.

Vickers metal. Many other attractive pewter vessels remain from this period: salts, beakers, loving cups in simple versions of silver design. But rival tablewares had a disastrous effect on mid-Georgian pewterers, many attempting to cut prices by using heavily leaded "thundercloud" alloys. Yet this was soon followed by a new era of widespread success. It is fascinating to trace how both these ancient alloys triumphed in the great "modern" industrial expansion of the late 18th century.

In pewter, the pioneer was John Vickers of Sheffield, who from 1769 began making a ware much like the early lead-free pewter, calling it Vickers white metal. Cream jugs, tobacco boxes, beakers, teapots have been found impressed with his name.

His stronger variant became important from the early 1790s; this was hard pewter or britannia metal, and by 1817 Sheffield alone had 73 makers, the Dixons being the most important.

Britannia metal, originally burnished bright as silver, is so like fine early pewter that the collector can distin-

Below: Vickers metal teapot and stand, late 1780s. Right: late 18th c. brass candlestick and pistol "strike-light".

guish it mainly by the way the machine age handled it.

For brass, the 18th century success story is largely associated with Birmingham, where brass was first made in 1740: 40 years later, the town used 1,000 tons of it every year. A much improved form of brass was available after 1738, and Georgians of the 1770s welcomed this lovely golden Emerson "spelter brass."

It was a splendid time for brass ware changing, like silver, from the mid century's lively rococo scrolls to the suave grace of the neo-classic vogue from the 1760s. Candlesticks and candelabra are found, and the saucer-shaped chamber candlestick, perhaps complete with a pair of snuffers and a cone extinguisher. Springs to make snuffers trim candles more cleanly came in 1749.

The smoker's wax-jack was popular: this has a flexible wax taper coiled round a central spool to burn with a safe, tiny flame. The pistol-shaped strike-light is a welcome find, too, as are brass and pewter pipe stoppers, snuff boxes and snuff rasps.

Matthew Boulton of Birmingham, 1728 to 1809, was a

leading figure in late 18th century factory achievement; he was renowned for ormolu – a refined, gilded brass used for ornaments, candelabra and lavish furniture mounts. By then, casting methods had improved. Improved rolling mills could flatten it into thin level sheets and improved steel in new stamping machines could shape and pattern it.

The early years of the 19th century saw power-driven machines rolling and stamping brass and britannia metal. Embossed surface patterns could be included – on many drawer handles, for instance – and repetitive perforations for small furniture galleries, but often cast ornament was preferred. Cast handles and feet became important details added to brass and britannia metal hollow ware shaped by spinning. For this, the flat plate was held in a lathe against a rotating wooden block. The careful collector looks for tiny tell-tale spiralling lines inside the vessel.

Not only brass kettles but all kinds of attractive hearth-side trivets date to this period – for kettles or for the tea-time britannia metal muffin dish, which would require

---

Below: pierced brass trivet, 1801. Right: cast brass chimera door stop, c. 1800; britannia metal covered jug, 1820s.

a small cinnamon dredger or muffineer. A patent of 1774 introduced the long favoured manner of keeping tea or breakfast urn hot by putting a bar of fire-heated iron into a central, vertical box inside it.

Regency brilliance. So much was happening to these alloys around the turn of the century, and into Regency and late Georgian years, that it is a wonderful period for the collector. Specialist collections include, for example, the scores of different brass emblems carried in their annual processions by village friendly societies which proliferated after an Act of 1793. Buttons challenge the collector to recognise and date the different ways their shanks were fitted.

Around the house, door-stops had become necessary after a self-closing door mechanism was introduced in 1775. At first, the "door porter" was a little ornament on a long handle, but from the 1790s a flatback shape was placed close against the door, whether dull half-bell or lively neo-classic lion, sphinx or chimera: these were followed in the 1820s and 1830s by horses, hounds,

celebrity figures and the early Victorians' favourite bird-and-snake. More surprising is the late arrival of the brass door-knocker, seldom dating earlier than Regency and now widely reproduced.

Britannia metal by then was enormously popular, too. A teapot, for instance, might be cast in a complicated, costly, many-part mould, but often the collector finds a vessel thinly spun or shaped by stamping, almost overwhelmed by the weight of cast ornament of vine or shells or oak leaves. Melon-shaping and turned-over edges strengthened the thin metal.

Lamps and candles. All the paraphernalia of early 19th century lighting has great appeal. Candlesticks in both alloys changed from severe neo-classic outlines to renewed flamboyance. They included thick-stemmed, straight telescopic sticks (patented 1796); bedroom sticks with tall glass shades explain the long-handled extinguisher.

Lamps ranged from the classic Roman floating-wick style to the Swiss-patented Argand lamp of the early 1780s. The period's sluggish vegetable and fish oils led to

---

Below: early 19th c. brass chamber candlestick, britannia metal candelabrum, 1825. Right: britannia metal tea ware.

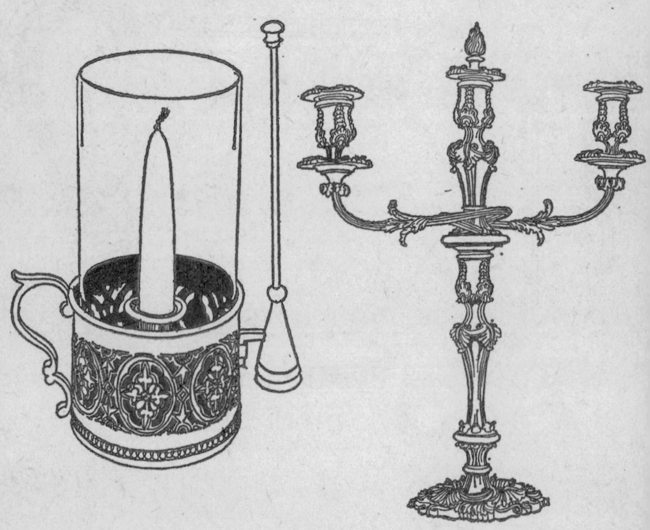

designs with urn-shaped fonts above the projecting burners. The moderator lamp with a regulated oil flow came in 1836. Meantime, dangerous benzine had been discovered in 1825 but paraffin came only in 1861.

The Victorian home. Revived rococo exuberance, lavish naturalistic flower and vine ornament, and contrasts of matt and burnished surfaces enabled brass and britannia metal to hold their own in the bright, cluttered Victorian home. As in china, the typical britannia metal teapot and matching vessels for coffee, milk and sugar were in the long-necked, heavy-bodied outline. Spout and feet tended to sag or sprawl but were rich in detail.

Even the fireside fender and poker, tongs and shovel – the "brasses" that were "done" each dawn by an under housemaid – shared the current enthusiasm for naturalistic flora and fauna. In 1838, however, A. W. N. Pugin, 1812 to 1852, the Gothic architect, became Birmingham's first designer of art brass and his Medieval Court at the 1851 Great Exhibition started a lasting interest in antique brass. At a more popular level, both alloys appeared

among pairs of figures sold as cheap chimney ornaments, which include miniature replicas of household furnishings. Many more of these were made in enormous quantities by specialists for dolls and dolls' houses.

The old leaded soft pewter continued in tavern pots and the like, but the cheapest pewter and lead castings were billies-and-charlies. Medallions and figurines in imagined ancient style were made and "discovered" in the Thames mud by William Smith and Charles Eaton. Revealed as fakes by 1858, they are now collected.

Horsebrass caution. Horsebrasses are so widely collected that they demand a section, although very few date any earlier than mid Victorian times. Many sold today (single-

Below: 1826 lidless tavern pot. Right: horse brasses of the 1880s are well finished and display a wide range of subjects.

piece castings in common industrial brass) betray their newness by a careless finish and artificially induced signs of wear bearing no relation to the way they were displayed.

Ever since Roman days, men have sought protection for their horses by dazzling the evil eye. The forehead face piece, for instance, was a domed latten disc by the 18th century, a cast, hand-finished sun with serrated edge from the 1820s, then appeared with drilled perforations until the 1870s when it was shaped by a single stamping in thin rolled brass, which was finished at first with very careful hand-filing.

Similar changes in production methods can be traced in

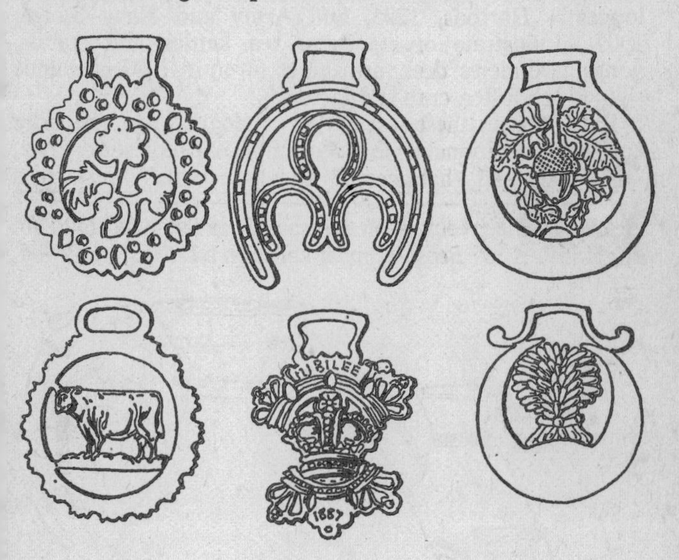

a collection of the most familiar martingale brasses – at York Castle Museum, for example. The collector notes, too, a late Victorian change in subject to many lacking the association with a driven horse or its owner and to souvenir portraits.

Art wares. The collector must recognise the colour and feel of his brass and this applies to every aspect of late Victorian metal work.

Even the name Queen Anne was misleadingly given to tablewares in silver style with vertical reeding on the lower half of the body of the piece.

Most interesting here are some of the late Victorian and Edwardian art wares. Two recently re-published catalogues – Harrods, 1895, and Army and Navy Stores, 1907 – illustrate ornate brass tea kettles and stands, gongs, jardinières, desk furnishings (even in 1907 inkstands shaped as lobster, crab and tortoise).

Illustrated in these fascinating catalogues, too, are more confusing traditional styles for example of candlestick, trivet, table lamp and "hammered" and "crocodile" brass trays

Below: Irish haycock spirit measures, pewter, 1820 to 1840.
Right: W. A. S. Benson copper kettle on a brass stand, 1905.

Britannia metal appeared in everything from toast racks to tea and coffee sets, including some traditional Georgian designs.

The old soft pewter was still in demand for ice pudding moulds, made to open and turn out any undercut shape. But soft pewter was specially welcomed by late Victorian aesthetes.

Interest was renewed when a Past-Master Pewterer became Lord Mayor of London in 1885 and included a craft display in the Lord Mayor's Show. Books on old pewter followed – and fakes.

A. L. Liberty introduced Tudric pewter in 1902. Edwardian ware shows both functional shapes of the Dresser school and rhythmical new-art contortions of flower and leaf, items ranging from soup tureen to fruit dish, from tea caddy to flower candlestick. In a period that approved expanses of dazzling, flawless brass, and might cover a britannia metal tankard with glossy nickel, there was much to recommend this gentle-toned, time-honoured and very collectable ware.

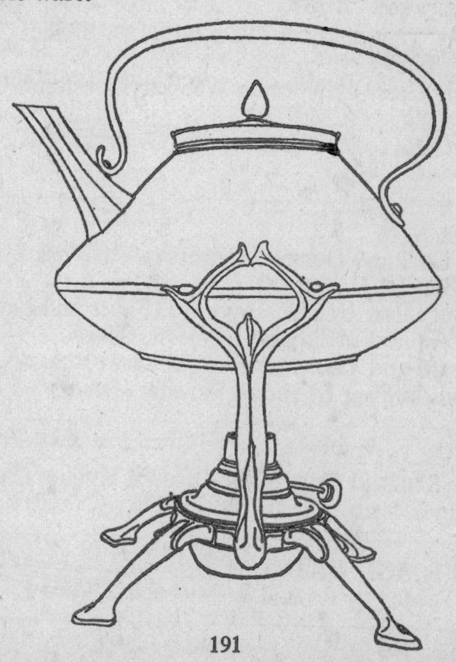

For Further Reading

FURNITURE
Encyclopaedia of Furniture by Joseph Aronson (Batsford)
World Furniture (Paul Hamlyn)
Old English Furniture by Therle Hughes (Lutterworth)

PORCELAIN
English Ceramics by Stanley Fisher (Ward Lock)
An Illustrated Encyclopaedia of British Pottery and Porcelain by Geoffrey A. Godden FRSA (Barrie and Jenkins)

POTTERY
World Ceramics (Paul Hamlyn)

GLASS
Collectors' Dictionary of Glass by E. M. Elville (Country Life)
Collecting Glass by Norman Webber (David and Charles)
Victorian Glass (H.M.S.O.)
English Glass for the Collector by G. Bernard Hughes (Lutterworth)

SILVER
English Civil and Domestic Silversmith's Work by Charles Oman (H.M.S.O.)
Huguenot Silver by J. F. Hayward (Faber and Faber)
Three Centuries of English Domestic Silver by Bernard and Therle Hughes (Lutterworth)
Old English Silver by Judith Banister (Evans)

SHEFFIELD PLATE
Antique Sheffield Plate by G. Bernard Hughes (Batsford)
Victorian Electro-plate by Shirley Bury (Country Life)

PEWTER AND BRASS
British Pewter by Ronald F. Michaelis (Ward Lock)